PENGUIN BOOKS

# Rescue 194

Chief Petty Officer Aircrewman Jay O'Donnell joined the Royal Navy in 1991. He qualified as one of a handful of Search and Rescue Divers in 2005. He's now stationed at RNAS Culdrose in Cornwall, flying with 814 Naval Air Squadron aboard Merlin anti-submarine helicopters. He was awarded the Queen's Gallantry Medal for the rescue of the crew of the MSC *Napoli*.

# Rescue 194

## CPO AIRCREWMAN
## JAY O'DONNELL QGM

PENGUIN BOOKS

# PENGUIN BOOKS

Published by the Penguin Group
Penguin Books Ltd, 80 Strand, London WC2R ORL, England
Penguin Group (USA) Inc., 375 Hudson Street, New York, New York 10014, USA
Penguin Group (Canada), 90 Eglinton Avenue East, Suite 700, Toronto, Ontario, Canada M4P 2Y3
(a division of Pearson Penguin Canada Inc.)
Penguin Ireland, 25 St Stephen's Green, Dublin 2, Ireland (a division of Penguin Books Ltd)
Penguin Group (Australia), 250 Camberwell Road,
Camberwell, Victoria 3124, Australia (a division of Pearson Australia Group Pty Ltd)
Penguin Books India Pvt Ltd, 11 Community Centre,
Panchsheel Park, New Delhi – 110 017, India
Penguin Group (NZ), 67 Apollo Drive, Rosedale, Auckland 0632, New Zealand
(a division of Pearson New Zealand Ltd)
Penguin Books (South Africa) (Pty) Ltd, 24 Sturdee Avenue,
Rosebank, Johannesburg 2196, South Africa

Penguin Books Ltd, Registered Offices: 80 Strand, London WC2R ORL, England

www.penguin.com

First published 2011

I

For more information about the Royal Navy's
global operations to defend the UK's
interests and acting as a force for good in the
world, please visit www.royalnavy.mod.uk

Set in 12.5/14.75pt Garamond MT Std
Typeset by Jouve (UK), Milton Keynes
Printed in England by Clays Ltd, St Ives plc

ISBN: 978-0-141-04109-4

www.greenpenguin.co.uk

Penguin Books is committed to a sustainable
future for our business, our readers and our
planet. This book is made from paper certified
by the Forest Stewardship Council.

# Contents

# Author's Note

The Royal Navy's Search and Rescue capability starts and ends as a form of military tasking. Rescuing civilians, be they sailors on yachts or on tankers, or walkers and climbers, or any other related emergencies, are ancillary tasks to the role that SAR plays within the Royal Navy's operations.

*Rescue 194* tells only one story of the many aspects of life in the Royal Navy, my own and that of other members of 771 Squadron. I never forget that I am a proud serving member of Her Majesty's Armed Forces and that many of my comrades and colleagues in all branches of the services face a far more dangerous and traumatic day, in combat zones such as Afghanistan, than I do when I board an aircraft to fly into the air above Cornwall.

I want to dedicate this book to the strength and courage of those serving abroad, and to the memory of those who fell in the service of their country.

And to my dad, who I felt was with me throughout those testing hours on the *Napoli* lifeboat.

Lastly to Sean 'Freddy' Krueger, who died 'doing his job', 7 July 2010. RIP mate.

# Prologue: The *Express Samina*

Chris ripped the door back and the heat inside the cab rushed out into the cold night outside, the pungent smell of aircraft fuel mingling with the salty Mediterranean air that poured in. I shuffled out of my low seat towards the open doorway of the Sea King Mk 6 and knelt by the side of the cab, peering down at the water below. A glimmer of light over in the far east lifted shadows out of the sea, greys and deep blues seeming to grow out of the thick blackness. Chris – the Observer and aircraft commander, as well as the winch op – spoke clearly over the intercom: 'We're nearly over the scene now, let's start looking out for any survivors, or anything else we can see out there.'

The roar of the rotor blades beating above my head was kept at bay by the well-fitting headset. With a microphone clipped to the front of my helmet, I could speak to everyone on board as well as hear clearly what was being said – not that there was much to report, as nothing from the shipwrecked *Express Samina* was visible below.

'It'll be a lot easier to see down there when dawn breaks,' I said. 'It's hard to see anything right now.' I didn't bother saying 'sir' when addressing Chris, no one

I

does when speaking to officers in the helicopters; if any of us did, it would slow down what has to be a fast – and sometimes frank – exchange of views.

From up front in the cockpit, one of the pilots chipped in: 'We've got some lights out in front of us. Fishing boats perhaps. Nothing bigger than that.'

Chris was in his seat opposite the door where I squatted, his eyes fixed on the radar screen in front of him. 'There's Gary coming in now, they're circling the boats below, they must have seen some survivors.'

No need for us to get in their way while they got on with the job, so we moved off starboard. I carried on looking down continuously for anything that might be a life raft or maybe some survivors gathered together with floatation devices. It was too dark to see individuals just yet, unless they had some sort of flares or reflective devices on them, but a group together might stand out.

An hour before midnight, the Greek passenger ferry *Express Samina* had capsized and sunk near the island of Paros, in the Aegean, going down in a little over half an hour. With the 500 people on board now in the water it was vital that any rescue was carried out as soon as possible because, we learned, the angle of the hull in the water had made it impossible to launch the lifeboats, while inflatable life rafts had blown away in the strong winds before those fortunate enough to grab one of the few life preservers could reach them. There was, though, one unexpected bit of good fortune in the unfolding tragedy. The Sea King helicopters of 814 Naval Air Squadron, on board HMS *Invincible* and RFA *Fort George*, were in the area and ready to answer the desperate call for help. We were airborne less than an hour after being shaken from our beds.

Every second counts when people are in the water, even in somewhere as seemingly benign as the Med. There's the probability of hypothermia setting in, as someone in the water loses their body temperature much faster in water than they would do on land; if the water is at, say, 10°C, they might expect to die in about an hour if they had no protection like a wetsuit or anything of that sort. The people down below us had already been in for a lot longer than that, because we'd been radioed from the ship as we were flying north to give us full details on what to expect; the ferry had gone down in a matter of minutes, and most of the passengers had no more than a quarter of an hour to get off the sinking ferry.

A voice from one of the *Invincible*'s aircraft came over the radio. It was Lieutenant Gary Milton, the commander of the SAR duty aircraft, saying, 'We've located some survivors on a rock, and Nick's going down to start bringing them up.' Nick Hipkin was one of the Aircrewmen from *Invincible*.

We listened in as Gary and his co-pilot radioed back what they could see below them – it was useful for us to know what sort of condition the survivors were in and what they might be able to tell all of us about any rescue craft there might be out there. 'Look at them down there,' we heard one of the pilots say. 'How could they survive that long?'

Along with hypothermia, one of the major dangers for a shipwrecked person in the water is panic: there they are in the dark, pushed around by the waves, with no prospect of rescue, and it doesn't matter who they are – panic is very likely to overtake anyone in a situation like that unless they've been trained to deal with it. It's a deadly enemy – someone in that state stops thinking clearly, calmly assessing their situation, and they start to consider – and do – desperate things. And if you're the one who goes in to rescue them, that's when problems can arise.

The two crews from the *Invincible* – who we were constantly in touch with whenever they, or we, came across somebody in the water so as to help pinpoint where to search next – had come across a small group of people hanging on to a big rock in the water. It must have seemed a good idea to them to climb on there but all that happened was that, with the waves battering them and the rock, those at the bottom kept trying to climb over those above them, hoping to get away from the waves that were threatening to pull them down into the water, to be lost in the darkness, never to be seen again. The two helicopters sat in the dark sky above them – one in the hover position over the rock, the other hanging back to give the duty aircraft some room to work, but close enough to come in to help if needed – and counted a dozen or more people crowded on their bleak shelter. None of these people had survival equipment of any sort with them – they were lucky they'd dragged themselves on to this rock, and there they were, while the sea greedily sucked at them, trying to take them back, one by one.

Nick was winched down to the rock. The women-and-children-first thing was obviously on his mind but certainly not on the survivors' minds, as grown men were climbing over each other, screaming and kicking and punching their way to that winch hook – which is only human nature. If they got near him, Nick fought back, because he was there to take the weakest first, the ones who had almost no chance of making it, and then come back down to take up the rest. So he punched men off him, trying to rescue the people that he obviously wanted to select, while the stronger ones fought each other as well as him, trying to get off first. It would have seemed weird to someone watching – punching someone you later save – but that's how best to deal with panicking people. The crew packed as many survivors as they possibly could into the first aircraft: they just kept going, keeping an eye on the weight, fuel and power; luckily they weren't too far away from the carrier so they could keep filling the cab up till the last minute, almost. Nick carried on, lifting people off, and didn't stop until he'd finished. The two helicopters returned to *Invincible* and refuelled before setting off again.

Chris was on the radio to Gary Milton to see what they'd learned from the survivors – if anything.

'They're telling us there didn't seem to be anything like enough lifejackets or life rafts for the people on board the ferry,' he told Chris. 'None of them had anything to help them. There was a British girl among the survivors' – later we learned that there were two of them – 'and she said that the ship had gone down so quickly that there hadn't been time for anyone to find a lifejacket or launch a life raft'.

By now I found it easier to see below us, because it was starting to get light. I spotted something and signalled to Chris to look too; it was probably just debris of some kind – I couldn't see anything that looked like a person, but we had to check. Chris nodded. 'I see it too, Jay, that looks like something that needs checking out,' and he spoke to the pilot: 'Take us down.' As we circled round and down, I clipped myself on to the winch. Once we were over whatever it was, I swung out over the side of the cab, the winch cable snapping taut as I hoisted myself out over the open air. My feet were still touching the side of the cab and I pushed away at the same time as Chris signalled to me, talking all the while to the guys up front to get them to keep a steady position, and lowered me down.

I didn't feel tense as I got closer to the object in the water. I could see it was a lifejacket and not a body. It looked empty to me, though I wanted to be sure there was no one hanging below it in the water and signalled to Chris to keep lowering me down to just above the surface so that I could grab it. There was no way of knowing whether or not it had been used; the straps weren't ripped but were just dangling loose, so I leant down and scooped it out of the water. I indicated to Chris to bring me up, and chucked the jacket into the back of the helicopter before disconnecting from the winch and turning back to stare out over the water below once more.

Two hours went by, two hours during which most of the survivors who were splashing around either had been rescued or had perished, while we were swooping down to pick up lifejackets, pieces of orange material, any debris we could see floating about – we felt we had to investigate every single one, if only to make sure that we didn't leave something for someone else to come past and assume was a victim in the water. We were dropping down and island-hopping from outcrop to outcrop, picking up loads of different jackets and other stuff floating about in the waves and on the rocks.

'There,' one of the pilots called, his voice urgent, 'out front, a life raft.' From the cabin behind him, Chris and I craned our necks to peer forward and, sure enough, there was a life raft. But as we flew in over the top we could see it was empty; well, not empty, exactly, just a bundle of shoes in the middle of the raft – otherwise it was totally deserted. I felt a shiver run up my spine; this was more than weird, it was downright spooky; what had happened to the people? It was like being in a movie where something catastrophic has occurred and left no survivors to talk to, to ask what's going on.

As the sun rose higher, this was something we all felt, until one of us said it: 'Where is everyone? Where has everyone gone to?' Sitting by the open door of the helicopter, with the sun warming me up a bit, I started to get a horrible feeling – were there any survivors at all? Little information on what other rescuers and searchers were finding was forthcoming from the Greek side so we only knew what the lads from *Invincible* had found. But I didn't voice my feeling as I thought we had to find *someone* alive out there.

'There, down there, there's someone in the water.'

For a fraction of a second hope surged through me but I was soon disappointed. I immediately knew it was a body, floating face down, but the others weren't so sure.

'I'm sure it is, look, you've got the head to the left, legs to the right, a white T-shirt.' There was a moment's pause.

'Yeah, wait a bit, could be, could be,' I heard over the intercom. We dropped down – we were flying along at about 500 feet or so to have a good view of the area – to run in at forty feet. Sure enough, there was our first casualty, bobbing about a bit in the waves as we got closer. 'How's he look?' asked one of the pilots. 'Has he seen us?' I killed off their optimism: 'He's dead, he has to be. He's not moving at all, and he's face down.' There was silence for a while.

'What are you going to need to recover him, Jay?' Chris asked. We acted like this was a rescue, even though we both knew that whoever was down there was already dead; they'd been in the water too long for that to be in any doubt. I'd readied what I would need – a single-lift strop and a grabbit hook, something we'd normally use for hoisting stores or similar bulky items. I don't know why I took the hook; maybe I thought it would give me flexibility in whatever I had to do next. I clipped myself on to the winch and said, 'OK, I'm hooked up and ready,' to Chris, and he lowered me out from the airframe and down to the water; as I went down I could hear him talking to the pilot – 'Hold it there, no, five yards to the left' – so as to make sure we stayed in the correct hover position over the figure in the water. Chris's voice faded as the spray from the downwash reached me – now we have waterproof equipment that prevents that, but back then once we were out of the helicopter we relied on hand signals.

The sea was calm so the body wasn't moving about too much as I got closer to him. I slid into the water alongside him, signalling to Chris to pay out some extra cable for me to work with. I don't know his name to this day, but he was clearly one of the chefs on board because he was wearing standard chef's gear of blue-and-white check trousers, black boots and a white T-shirt. I could see immediately that he was lifeless.

At this point I'd just been down to my elbows in the sea so far, hanging on the wire pulling up lifejackets and stuff; as I slid in I instantly realized that it was colder than I'd expected and – more importantly – that I had no buoyancy at all, which up to that point hadn't mattered. I could have changed into my goon bag up in the aircraft, the green ones that seal around the neck and wrists so as to keep us watertight, but it might have been on my mind not to as we're only ever supposed to immerse them twice, because after that we write them off and then they're only good for use in training. Maybe it was because we were in the Med, and I assumed it'd be a lot warmer than the waters off Cornwall I was used to, and maybe it was because I'd had an argument with the survival-equipment clerk back on the *Invincible* about helping myself to some spare SE kit and only got half of what I wanted – getting an extra suit hadn't crossed my mind. So there I was in the water trying to get on with my job while breathing in sharply to deal with the cold. I hadn't inflated my lifejacket and in order to keep alongside the body was treading water like it was going out of fashion, and splashing round as I worked.

As he was dead, I had to concentrate on how to recover the body safely, and I started by observing him carefully. He was face down, probably in his late twenties or early thirties, dark-haired. He'd been in the water a couple of hours by this time and had obviously become very cold at some point because I could see he had folded his arms in tightly around himself as he'd tried to conserve his core-body temperature, and that's the position he'd died in. That must have been a few hours ago because rigor mortis had set in and his arms had frozen in that position. This was the first difficulty

I was going to have; somehow I would have to get his arms open enough to slip the primary strop over them so that he could be safely lifted out of the water. Since I had no buoyancy, as soon as I started trying to do this I was wrestling against his weight just to keep my own head above the water.

I'd just managed to prise his arms open a bit when they suddenly closed up on me. *Jesus* – what the hell was going on? I tried again, but every time I managed to get his arms a little further apart, they would close back into the position they'd been in – it was as if I was fighting with a dead body. I realized after a moment's thought that it was only because his arms had been locked by the onset of rigor, but initially it freaked me out.

To get a better chance of slipping the strop into the right place I thought it easiest to go underwater, so instead of trying from the side I would place the strop between his arms from the front and then slide it into place once I'd got the arm furthest away from me into the strop. I had to slide myself under him and at first I tried not to look at his face as I worked with him, but of course I had to anyway.

What came next still haunts me, although I wouldn't say it scared me. It's not because I'm trying to be macho about it; it's just that as with all aircrew in the Royal Navy I've been trained so hard there usually isn't room to feel fear. I'd take anything as just another chance to look at some more options. There is nothing unexpected because we've considered every eventuality, that's how we like to think of it.

Still, on this occasion I'd been fighting with the body, which had been bad enough, and then slipped down under the water; I'd taken a large gulp of air, and I had swum into position underneath him and was under the water fiddling with the strop when I looked up and saw his eyes were open and – literally, like in a horror film – were completely black, sightlessly staring back at me. I'd seen bodies in the past – admittedly, not in such close proximity as that – but nothing like this: no definition to the pupil, the whole eye – just black. *What the hell was that?* I wanted to rear back; it was as if he was watching me from behind this deathly mask, but I blinked hard and tried to clear my head. Get on with bringing the guy home. I signalled to Chris and the winch wire started tightening; I wrestled with the body a little more before it got clear of the water and we both started being winched back up to the aircraft, water pouring off in sheets as we rose higher and higher.

Chris had seen what was going on and winched us both slowly and carefully back up to the aircraft. All the time we were going up I was holding on tight to the guy, aware that his belt was likely to give way at any moment, because of its being so wet and loose. It was my fear that he would slip and fall out of my grasp; alive or dead, you don't want to drop anybody from the winch as we're approaching the aircraft – it just doesn't get much worse than that, the impact's horrendous. I checked again and again that the strop was tight around him, but he was a dead body and therefore wouldn't – couldn't – do anything to help. I had no idea whether or not the strop would stay on him given that at any moment his arms might suddenly flip upwards and the strop would slide up and off him.

We reached the aircraft and I swung inside and grabbed the body, and finally, just as I heaved him into the cab, his belt split and I fell backwards with his dead weight tumbling in after me. We ended up in an undignified heap. I rolled him off and, winded, pulled him down to the back of the aircraft and away from the door.

'Jay! Jay!' Chris shouted over the noise of the engines. 'Are you all right? Are you okay? Are you injured at all?' He looked alarmed.

'I'm all right,' I tried to reassure him, 'a bit emotional but let's get on. Press on with the search.'

I plugged myself back into the aircraft's comms The co-pilot craned round from the cockpit, and said to Chris, 'Is he okay?'

'No.' Chris shook his head. 'He's definitely dead. There's no point doing CPR because rigor mortis has set in, he's been gone for hours.'

But Chris was distracted. The look on his face suggested he was more concerned about the state I was in than our new passenger. I didn't get it. I must have looked puzzled because Chris nodded towards my midriff. I looked down. I was soaked in red. It looked like blood. It was everywhere, on my gloves, all down my front, all down my legs – my overalls were just wrecked. I rapidly patted down the places that might have been cut – my scalp, arms, legs – but I was certain I hadn't been hurt and sure enough nothing seemed wrong. I got up to take another look at the body, and then I realized what had happened.

'It's just paint,' I told Chris, pointing to a extinguished red flare gripped tight in the chef's lifeless hand. 'It's flare paint of some sort that's come off him.' The dead man had gone overboard with nothing else to help in the water but a single flare. And he'd obviously tried to use it, perhaps to see rather than be seen in the darkness. Maybe even to keep himself warm by heating the water around him as the cold started to seep into his bones. Poor bastard. It must have been too dark in the water to see that colour, and as I'd been pressed up against the chef as I brought him up on the winch it had rubbed off on me, while I was too busy making sure he didn't slip off the winch to worry about anything like that.

We pushed on. After a while we spotted a second person in the water. I don't remember who saw the body first but as we went into the hover, Chris conning the pilot into position right above the spot, I realized that it was a woman.

'You all right? Chris asked. 'Happy?'

I nodded. 'Yep, fine, let's go for it,' and down I went. She was in her late forties, maybe early fifties, and

I noticed her earrings; she looked more like a tourist than a local. She was quite large and also half naked – she didn't have any top on or anything, her clothes were hanging around her neck and waist. I had to struggle a bit with her body to get the strop round her and, as with the chef, her eyes were lifeless black holes.

Once Chris had raised us both back up to the aircraft, we moved her to the back; only this time I went a bit weird. Perhaps because she was more vulnerable than the chef, being half naked; anyway I decided I had to give her back some dignity, so I started to dress her again, by putting her bra back on. What I didn't plan to do though was to talk to her at the same time, which is what I did, apologizing as I did so, saying I was sorry I hadn't got to her in time to bring her out alive, explaining things just as if she were able to hear what I was doing as I put her clothes back on. The totally black eyes were also freaking me out a bit and I tried to close them by pulling down her eyelids, but as the muscles had gone rigid this didn't work. I carried on talking to her, explaining what I was doing, dressing her, and I guess this must have looked very strange to Chris; but he said nothing about it to me.

The helicopter was moving on to search in the next area; we were working to a grid system now that the Greeks had launched a Hercules, and were organizing the rescue by directing all of the ships and aircraft in the area from this airborne base.

As we flew on, something made me look back to the

rear of the helicopter. We hadn't strapped the bodies in, as not only were we trying to move as fast as possible, hoping that we'd come across survivors, but it is near impossible to strap in a rigid body once rigor mortis has set in. If I'd thought that lifting bodies out of the water with their open sightless eyes was bad enough, what I saw now was worse than any nightmare Hollywood could dream up. The two bodies lay there with their open black eyes, shaking with the vibration of the aircraft, and, as I watched, thick froth began to bubble up from their mouths and out of their noses.

'What the hell . . .' I saw Chris grimace at the sight of it.

There are protocols on a flight and one of them is that we don't all talk over each other. It's no good having someone shouting in your ear while you're trying to make a tricky decision. But on this occasion both Chris and I blurted something out that made the pilots start in their seats.

'What's that? What's going on?'

Chris explained: 'I guess maybe it's a mixture of dirty seawater and blood being shaken out of their lungs by the juddering in the cab,' but he didn't need to add how when we had first seen the foam coming out of their mouths and noses how horribly scary it had looked.

We came across our third body. I went down again, and it was by now almost automatic; I had switched off, my brain said this is becoming all too much and it just went on to auto. It was a man, older than the first one, and he was heavy and cumbersome to move about in the water. It didn't help that the cold was really starting to bite. The searching went on, but it was awful; everywhere we went there were bodies, and I went down on the winch a few more times to recover each one. The process was numbing, but then so was the intense cold. I felt no better once I was back in the cab with the door open, the wind blowing and me sitting there soaking wet, bitterly regretting that, in the scramble to get airborne, I'd pulled on nothing more substantial than a thin flight suit. But the big twin-engine Sea King was approaching her limit too.

'We're getting a bit low on fuel,' Chris announced to all of us. 'Let's go back.' It's everyone's job on board to keep track of fuel and airtime, but it was Chris's call to end the search. The helicopter swung round on a new heading towards *Invincible*, the carrier acting as the command-and-control centre for the Royal Navy helicopters during the whole operation. We radioed in ahead so as to let them know we were on our way and to prepare them for our gruesome cargo.

We touched down on deck on Zero Spot, ahead of the carrier's island. Teams ready to receive casualties – stretcher-bearers and medical personnel – were upon us as soon as we threw back the cabin door. Aircraft had been coming in with survivors and also bodies at different times during the morning, as all the bodies and the survivors came on to *Invincible*. We were aware that we should definitely de-conflict both; as far as I'm aware that happened, but there were people all over the bloody place; the deck was busier than ever. There were helicopters all down the carrier's landing strip; One Spot, right at the front of the aircraft carrier, is now called Zero Spot, with the take-off ramp to one side and the end of the Alaskan Highway on the other (the Alaskan Highway runs down the blind side of the carrier's superstructure, away from the airstrip). We touched down and I clearly remember the faces of the guys who came to the doors of the helicopter. They were quite shocked, because, I guess, although they realized they were picking up bodies, nothing prepared them for what they were about to see, and, unlike us, they hadn't been carried along on adrenaline.

Years later I was in a nightclub in Helston and an Air Engineer from our squadron came up to me. 'All right, Jay?' I didn't really know him very well. I knew he was one of the engineers but I never really got to know him – some you do, some you don't; but I couldn't figure out why he suddenly decided he wanted a chat with me. And then it came out, because after a few minutes he said, 'Ah, you did that job didn't you, that SAR job, the *Express Samina*.'

'Yeah, I did, I remember that pretty well.'

'Yeah,' he said, in a way that made me look at him a little more attentively, 'so do I. It really screwed me up, that did.'

I was surprised not so much that the incident had affected him – after all, I still had dreams about it myself – but that he told me there, in a nightclub of all places. He went on, obviously keen to talk to me about this.

'When we returned to port I had to go and get some counselling. I never told the Navy, didn't want them thinking me a wacko, I never even told my family.'

'Wow, it hit you that hard, did it?'

'Yeah. When I came to the aircraft and saw you covered in red, I thought it was blood at first, you was piss-wet through, white-faced too because you was cold and exhausted. And then you was handing down these dead bodies, froth coming out of their mouths and noses, their eyes open, all this red everywhere . . .' He tailed off. The music thumped away in the background but I was suddenly shoved back there, myself, by his recollections.

'It all just blew me away. I went into mechanical mode, getting on with the job as expected, loading the bodies from the aircraft on to stretchers but inside I was reeling, everything churning away, I couldn't believe what I was seeing.' He paused. 'You know, we engineers all take the piss, it's part of the banter, we have a go at you lot: oh, you aircrew, you don't do anything, you just go up and buzz about having a laugh. I suppose I half believed that. But that day on *Invincible* changed everything for me. It's like it's on a reel in my head; I never got over what I saw then.'

The *Express Samina* rescue stayed with me too, but my reaction to it was rather different. Despite the grim

nature of the task, I'd found something that I really felt
I wanted to do more than anything else since I'd first
stepped on board a Sea King. Going down on the winch,
getting into the water, pulling people – hopefully alive –
out; I had a new goal. I now set my sights on graduating
from one of the Navy's toughest training programmes.
I was going to be a Search and Rescue Diver

# PART ONE

PART ONE

# 1. Ready to Fly

You don't just turn up in a Royal Navy recruiting office and say, I'd like to be an SAR Diver please; it took me years – and some blood along with the sweat and tears – to get there. However, ever since I was a boy I'd known I wanted to join the Royal Navy, and I had always had an interest in helicopters – but I never thought I'd end up flying in them. My training had set me up as an engineer, and I'd started out working on the cabs before I ever got a chance to fly in one of them.

Growing up in the West Country, I'd joined the Sea Scouts and then, at the age of thirteen, the Sea Cadets. I loved sailing and a chap in our village used to take me out regularly in his boat. It was thanks to him I had my first taste of life in the service – he arranged for a small group of us from the Sea Cadets to spend the day out in HMS *Onyx*, one of the Navy's submarines.

We were taken through security to the dock, and gathered alongside some rough-looking men hanging around in some sort of little shelter – they were the submarine crew, returning from a night ashore, looking three sheets to the wind. A pass boat came across and picked us up to take us on the short trip across to HMS *Onyx*, which was moored on a buoy near the mouth of the harbour. *Onyx* was a diesel-powered submarine of the kind that's been phased out these days; it had last seen service during the Falklands War, when it was the only non-nuclear sub there. It was great to be on board but even to my teenage mind I knew it was only a Smartie tube that went under the water, and it didn't feel much bigger than that, either.

It was great to see how it operated. We dived and we snorted, which is when the submarine comes to just above periscope depth and the upper hatches are opened so they can suck in a massive amount of air down – while still staying submerged as they've not come to fin depth – to run through the engines because they needed air to charge the batteries, which had to be charged when the sub had to run silent, run deep. We surfaced and did all the drills, hoisting flags and stuff. We were out there for a while before the Captain said, oh, we've just had an emergency signal and I'm afraid we're going to have to drop you back at Plymouth as we're going to have to sail immediately. Oh, can you tell us where to, or what for? No, sorry. Now this might have been made up just for us but it was still pretty exciting for us boys to hear about.

It was a great day out and when I wrote to thank the Captain, he sent back a photograph of HMS *Onyx*, which I've still got today. I thought quite hard about going into submarines after that, but I wasn't won over and still preferred to think of my future career being closer to the airborne side of the Navy as my greater passion remained helicopters. I did wonder how people could live in such a confined close space.

Our family holidays were always spent in Cornwall, and we'd often go to Flambards, a large theme park in Helston. Flambards was a great place for any young boy to go to but it was even better for me as it was right next door to a Royal Naval Air Station, RNAS Culdrose – by coincidence, the helicopter station where 771 is based and where I work now. As a young lad I would stand and watch in awe as all kinds of helicopters launched and flew off, and I would pester my dad: 'Can't we go any closer? Can we go in there so I can see them better?' He would point to the twenty-foot-high fence topped with barbed wire that surrounded the place and tell me that no, we couldn't go in there.

I was always interested in mechanical things and spent a lot of time taking stuff apart. Presumably because it was next door to Culdrose, Flambards had a little store of parts from helicopters and I spent many happy hours poking about in the discarded pieces of machinery. Once I came across the nose of a Wessex and tinkered with that for what must have seemed like days to my family.

I joined the Royal Navy at seventeen; as it was a natural progression from the Sea Cadets it wasn't such a big transition – I already understood the way of life and had a sense of discipline. I stayed on at school after GCSEs for a year, taking A levels in maths, physics and technology; back then the Navy's manpower levels were higher than today's, so you applied to join but were told when they were ready to take you. After a year I got the call to come and join up; my parents wanted me to stay on at school and complete my A levels, but I was keen to get on and start what I knew would be the adventure of my life, so I was packed off at Teignmouth Station by my dad on 17 June 1991.

About the first thing I learned when I arrived at HMS *Raleigh* was that – like all Royal Navy bases – it was referred to as a ship, but it was land-based. A new recruit doesn't enter HMS *Raleigh*; he or she comes on board.

Once I'd been taken through the admission process, I joined the other recruits. To begin with, we were kitted out and then given our first stage of basic training. We were put into large rooms, thirty or more in each one, to develop a team ethos; a bit tough for us coming straight from home, living in each other's pockets like that. Everyone else who'd joined up at that time was new to me but I did know someone, Ryder Morley, who'd been in the Sea Cadets branch where I'd been, who'd joined the year before, so I had some idea of what to expect. To be honest, that first week wasn't too bad – nothing more than I'd anticipated. It was week two when it all changed, and that started with my hair being shorn. Then I was shown how to care for my uniform, keeping it ironed in just the right way, how to clean my clothes in the sink – there were no washing machines as we were too far down the food chain and we didn't get such luxuries until much later on. This isn't a particularly arduous process but it does sort out those who can cope with a disciplined military way of life from those who can't. I was also taught how to fire weapons and various other fundamental skills.

I did my basic eight-week military training at *Raleigh*; at the end of that time, I was ready to move on to my chosen specialist area.

In those days, they tried to fit new recruits into gaps in the Fleet, rather than give them the choice of career that they wanted to take up, as is the case now. At the age of seventeen, just like all the others who'd joined up with me, I didn't know how the world worked or how the Armed Forces worked. The Navy may have been an attractive place to be when I first went in, but it was quite strict and a lot of people found themselves railroaded into jobs they didn't want to do. I stood firm on my desire – those helicopters I'd seen shooting over my head at Flambards were still very much on my mind. At the Navy recruiting office I'd done really well in my maths test so the Navy wanted me to be an Artificer – which meant I'd have been an engineer on a ship, perhaps responsible for weapons; but I wanted to be involved with flying, so I opted to be an Air Engineer, a mechanic, and to work on helicopters. Up to this point, all I'd ever done was sit in the back of one of the machines when it was on the ground.

I moved on to HMS *Daedalus*, at Lee-on-Solent, the base for aviation training, especially engineering. I was there for just over six months, learning on Wessex 5s; every day I'd pull them apart, put them back together, putting pressure into the systems, testing everything as we went along. It never came into my mind to want to pilot the things; it just wasn't my inclination, which had always been towards engineering – taking things to pieces – it's just how my brain worked. Being in engineering, though, meant I got to see what everybody else in the helicopter business does, and the Aircrewman's role looked really tempting to me. There are only about 140 Aircrewmen these days in the whole Navy so it was very difficult to get into, but that only tempted me more. I thought, yes, that is the job for me, I want to be an Aircrewman, I want to be hanging out of the door, in the Commando role, I want to be operating the winch, that looked exciting. And that's why I joined the branch initially, so once I'd completed the course I was transferred from HMS *Daedalus* to HMS *Heron* at RNAS Yeovilton, and went on the Mk 4 Sea King.

I started in April 1992 with 707 Naval Air Squadron, HMS *Heron*, and in December that year I went on to a front-line squadron, 845 which became the longest serving British unit during the war in the former Yugoslavia.

In January 1993 I was dragged in and crash-drafted from 845 Naval Air Squadron to 846 NAS and told we were to be part of the UN peacekeeping force, UNPROFOR tasked with back-up and evacuation, so we'd be involved in real action not just training.

I was going out on HMS *Ark Royal* on a day and a half's notice. The *Ark Royal* had been recalled at immediate notice to Portsmouth from a training exercise in Norway. So although 846 and 845 were next door to each other in RNAS Yeovilton this meant that I had to complete a leaving routine from 845 and a joining routine to 846 in a matter of an hour or two. I was told to get kitted out and 'say goodbye to your parents'.

'How long am I going for?' I asked. 'Could be six months, could be a year.' Now this was my first time on an overseas posting and I hadn't really expected anything so dramatic, so soon, and for so long. I drew full front-line kit, fighting order and Arctic kit – basically two huge kit bags on top of all our other kit. I had to report at 1000 the following day, when the buses would arrive to take the whole squadron down to embark. As this was the very first time I had ever left home to – to all intents and purposes – go to war, I wanted to see my friends as well as say goodbye to my folks. I made my way home, found time to go out for a few jars with my mates, and went off to sea clutching my hangover the following morning.

After a time at sea staffing levels allowed me to rejoin 845 and the squadron was sent to Divulje barracks in Split, in Croatia, just the other side of the mountain range by the border. I did three tours out there, and although I probably shouldn't say it, as we were in a war zone, I had a good time. The UN had taken over and rebuilt a Croatian army barracks; 845 was assigned to quite a large building with its own compound in the far corner of the barracks, out of the way of everybody; nobody really knew what to do with us because although we'd come with Sea King Mk 4 helicopters we weren't the same as the rest of them, as we were Navy. There were loads of different nations in the barracks, and we were next door to the Cloggies – the Dutch – and the Norwegians and maybe some others, so even though we were all UN, we made sure that our compound was definitely British. We had quite a contingent with us, too: we had five flights on the squadron, with four aircraft, operating on the hard standing, with the French and the Croats in their own hangars. With a crew of three or maybe four for each aircraft and a full team of engineers, there were a lot of us and over the next few months the number of aircraft went up and soon we had pretty much the whole squadron over there, with just a couple of airframes back at Yeovilton for training. The pilots and aircrew rotated their duty, but we engineers were on a different watch so that we could keep each aircraft serviced and running. It wasn't the place for things to go wrong and there wasn't anywhere we could send the aircraft back to for repairs: it was us or nothing. We'd work on the aircraft at speed; we'd take off a gearbox, remove the rotors, strip everything down and put a new one in, test-fly it and have it ready the next morning, eight hours in all. Away from a war zone it can take days.

As ever we worked just as hard to make sure we

enjoyed ourselves. There was a little balcony on the building, and when we weren't on duty and it was hot enough – which it often was – we'd get out there to sun ourselves. The Junior Rates' bar was downstairs, the Senior Rates' bar upstairs, and we had some great parties there – perhaps that's why the place used to get a revamp at the end of every tour. The base was pretty secure; the whole place was surrounded with metal sheeting. Our quarters went down to the hard standing and our hangars were right opposite that, down on the water's edge, we had canoes and yachts and a rigid inflatable that had been donated to us, so of course in our off-duty time we'd go waterskiing. The Navy has always been really good at that, making the most of our down-time, so that no matter what we had to do when we were on duty we didn't go under with the stress of it all. The Army lads would be sent down to us after being in theatre for six months, for a week of chilling out before flying home to reality, and they'd be greeted by the sight of a boat going past with a Navy lad in shorts, waving as he skied past the jetty. They'd drop their bags and stand gobsmacked – 'Who the hell's that?' – as the boat made yet another pass, with a Jolly Jack Tar on some skis calling out, 'All right?'

The Banana Boat Club, as we called it, opened up to take all the Pongos – the Royal Navy name for the Army – out skiing. We knew they needed to relax a little after what was a pretty awful time; there wasn't much action in Split, but it was mad across the border. I managed to see that for myself after I'd been lying about in the sun a bit too much – I wasn't used to it, but as there was snow on the mountains it didn't seem such a bad idea. Some moles on my skin started to itch – I had one large one on my front and two on my back – and the medics said they should probably be removed, so I had to go to a hospital inland to have an operation to take them off. I was flown up by one of our aircraft to Gornji Vakuf, and then I was told I was going to be driven by a Royal Marine the rest of the way in a UN vehicle, that I'd be kitted out in full battle order, with Bergen and weapons, and that I'd need an Intelligence Briefing before we left. I asked why.

'Because there's currently believed to be ninety-two different warring factions in this area, different armies, different warlords running the different groups, so you'll need to know who you may run into and what to do if you do. As it is, you will have to ride shotgun for the driver to help him out.'

Oh . . . right. The field hospital was in the middle of nowhere, and it was inevitable of course that we got lost. So there we were, bimbling around in a white Land Rover in the middle of God-knows-where in a war zone, the bootneck and me, weapons all over the place at the ready. At one point we drove up to a checkpoint, something hastily assembled across the road, and I put my hand down by the side of the door, holding on to my gun, thinking that this is bad, we're well outnumbered here. I don't know which faction it was that was

hol
me
wet
could
aroun
UN w
didn't
tually f
out and
Marine t
his own
have to g
could mot
luck and we

sunbathing, cruising past the supermar
craft carrier's five deck, smoothing in
craft carrier's a bit of a divide
There's always last on – becaus
we're always last on – becaus
and as soon as we're not
manent leave. So I'm
Pongos and their
matically than
'Snipers
Oh
dif

The camp ... the open door. After I'd che ... wondering what the routine was going to be, I was told: 'Oh, you'll just catch scran if you're lucky, get across to the mess hall quickly. Dump your bag there' – pointing to the corner – 'and run over.'

I wondered why I had to run. Was this an Army thing? I'm Navy, I'm a WAFU – Weapons and Fuel User, the term used for anyone in the naval aviation world, although we like to explain it stands for Women Always Fancy Us: it distinguishes us from the Fish-Heads or Cod-Gobs or Skates or whatever other name the general sailor was called. They generally get really upset about us, as they never see the WAFUs doing much, just trawling about the deck, doing a bit of

ket on the air-
on all the women.
on a ship like that, as
e we fly on – and first off,
here they think we're on per-
not really used to the world of
rules, but I put it a bit more diplo-
that. 'What's the rush for?'

. If you move quickly, you can avoid them.'

great. Roadblocks, snipers – this was all a bit
erent to life down by the sea. So I took my helmet
and weapon and did as I was told – I legged it. In the
mess hall I was told to put my weapon in the rack by
the entrance, to remove my body armour and get a tray
of food. It was only when I was sitting down and had
taken my first mouthful that something crossed my
mind: is it right to eat before your operation? That's not
usual, is it? This could be bad news, couldn't it? And
another thing, something I hadn't mentioned to anyone: it was my twenty-first birthday, and here I was in
a camp in the middle of a war about to have an
operation – not exactly how I'd have planned it. I
rushed back over once I'd eaten and was going to ask,
am I going to have to wait for the operation, then, is
that why I've been allowed to eat, but I was told firmly
to hang around while they sorted out a team for me.

Finally someone comes to see me and I'm taken
down into the middle of the hangar and another tent.
At last there's a doctor but I don't get to ask him

anything – straight away he leaps in: 'Right we've got to cut those moles out. It seems the moles have roots on them, that's why they've got to go.' All this was a bit concerning – I thought it was just something on the surface that'd gone a funny colour, and now they're talking about digging about in me. He took a look at the one on my front and turned me round to prod and poke at the ones on my back. 'Which way do you want to do it first?' he said briskly.

'I don't care, the least painful.' And I added: 'You know I've just had some food?'

'Yes?'

'Generally you don't if you're just going to have an operation, do you?'

'Oh yes, but that's only if you're going to be put under – we don't do generals here, you're not getting a general anaesthetic, you'll be lucky if you get a local anaesthetic, you are in a war, you know.'

Yes, I didn't say, I appreciate that but I didn't think I was supposed to do it with a stick between my teeth.

I lay down and he sprayed something on my skin. A nurse standing beside the bed sympathetically put her hand in mine and I gripped it tightly as the doctor started slicing, and I tell you, that poor nurse's hand felt like dust at the end of it. It was agony – I couldn't even scream because it hurt too much. Horrendous, awful pain. Finally he was done and sprayed something else on me that made no difference to the pain levels, and then patched me up.

Just then I realized why I'd been lucky to have eaten already, and also not to have had a general anaesthetic before: one of the local ninety-two factions started shelling the base. It was all kicking off and the doctor and nurse just pulled me up – *owwww* – and set me off and running. 'It's just outside the camp at the moment, we're okay, but get yourself under cover.' It certainly didn't sound like it, as the missiles crumped and thumped around me. We're getting shelled in an operating theatre in a hangar, where I've just been cut open, in the middle of Bosnia, and it's my twenty-first birthday – great, this is a memorable day.

I made it back safely to the barracks at Divulje the following day and never set foot outside the base again.

It's always better in the air, and that's what happened for me next. I had known for a while now that what I was interested in doing was trying out for aircrew. I still had a long way to go before I could get there, as I had a number of tours to do first, but once I'd decided that's what I was interested in – and had told a few of the lads – my mind was made up. Next step, then, was to request a branch change, from engineering to aircrew.

Ahead of that request, though, there were certain protocols that had to be gone through to become an Aircrewman. Before I could even make a formal application I had to have passed my exam for Leading Hand, in my chosen trade of engineering, and to even get that far I had to have the relevant education qualifications, which in those days were quite strict. I did my engineering exam out in Bosnia and passed for promotion to Leading Hand, at which point I could then request to go on the Commanding Officer's Table as, to progress to aircrew, I would have to be recommended by my CO.

The CO's Table was very formal; it didn't matter that we were in a war zone, the process was going to be exactly the same as it had been practised over the years. I arrived in my best uniform and stood outside waiting to be called in to see the CO. The regulator – in my case a naval policeman – called me to attention, and I was marched in to salute the CO. He was stood behind a lectern – that's the table, oddly enough – and he heard my application.

The CO asked questions, such as why did I want to go for this role, how did I think it's going to affect me, what did I think I'd be doing in my role, what aircraft type interested me, all stuff that I enjoyed answering and which made sense to me. He just wanted to make sure I was making the request for the right reasons before he said, yes, and stepped forward to shake my hand and wished me good luck. 'I'll tell the rest of the boys that I've approved this, we'll get you flying,' which was great as being out in theatre was a perfect opportunity for me to get a lot of flying experience and really clock up some hours in the air. As soon as I was back in the PO – the Petty Officers' mess – the Chief Aircrewman grabbed me and said what I wanted to hear: 'Let me know when you're off watch and when you want to go flying.' Although we were busy when the aircraft needed servicing or repairing, there was nothing much to do once we went off watch: we'd either write a mailey, or polish our shoes or do light phys. Now I had an alternative – I could go flying. Once they knew that I wanted to go for aircrew, the guys would take me up when I wasn't on watch. They'd make sure I was sorted out legally, that I'd signed the indemnity form, and then we'd be off. Wartime offers some pretty amazing flying experiences and some of the things I did with them were just that. There are only a few things in life you can say you've done that other people have never done, like flying down the main street of Sarajevo. Unreal enough at the time, it just seems unbelievable to me thinking back now.

The crewmen then took me up flying as often as I wanted to, so on all my off-watch days I was in the back of the cab having a great time. We'd do training as well so that I knew what I'd face once I was on the Aircrewman's course. I practised winching someone up and down over the hard standing: this involved putting my mate 'Smokey' Robinson into a prickly bush, testing for accuracy of course; I quickly learned that there was a considerable downside as it was his turn afterwards. We had many trips out over – and into – Sarajevo as I got used to the experience of flying at very low levels.

Another time we were out practising some manoeuvres when a call came in for a rescue job. The pilot, Kevin Smith, who was decorated for his work in

Bosnia, was right-hand-seat flying the aircraft while I was in the left-hand seat, with a load of guys in the back, along with our own crew. One of them was an Army major; I can't remember who the other guys were – maybe it was one of the experience flights we ran, trying to keep troops happy when they were in the barracks with us – an aircraft and a number of hours were set aside specifically for this. Because this call came through when we were airborne and available, we had to go and carry out a rescue. I said to Kevin: 'Sir, I'm left-hand seat, what am I going to do here, do you want me to move?'

He said, 'No, stay there, you're all right, you can use this experience to learn from,' so the other pilot remained in the back while Kevin flew us out there. We had to fly out to the island, which was called Bo, or something like that, where a hang-glider had creamed into the side of a cliff. He was apparently precariously hanging on a ledge and we went searching for him. As we approached the cliff-face, Kev got me to hold the throttle while we circled around. Kev is one of those guys that trusts you to do the right thing and so gives you the confidence to do it because you trust him, but let's not forget I was just an Aircraft Engineer who'd had between ten and fifteen minutes' hands-on flying experience up till then. I certainly didn't forget. He let me take it right up to the point of the hover, at which point he took over; there was nowhere to land that was close enough for anyone in the back to get to, so

Kev – I couldn't believe it – flew the aircraft close enough to the cliff-face, with the door open, with the crewman conning him in. He must have had the aircraft step a foot, half a foot, from the cliff-face – the blades would have been the same – so that the major and a couple of lads could jump out of the aircraft in the hover on to the cliff-face to try and sort this hangglider out. We got him on board the aircraft – it was a bit of a nightmare because his kit started to blow around, which could have had dramatic consequences if it had tangled up in the rotors – and flew him to a hospital.

That was my first experience of an aviation rescue and what a brilliant experience it was. If I'd ever harboured any doubts at all about what I'd chosen to do, they were blown away now as I knew more than ever that what I wanted was to be on a Search and Rescue job like this, to be aircrew. This, I thought to myself, was the business.

# 2. Search and Rescue

Search and Rescue in the aviation world began as a military necessity in the First World War, when planes returning from sorties over the North Sea crashed in the sea off Britain. The first rescue involving a ditched plane was achieved thanks to a pigeon. The crew of an aircraft in 1917 ditched after being shot down by the Zeppelin it had gone out to attack in the first place; communications not being what they are now, the crew of the downed plane had to send details of their location via carrier pigeon. Today, the body of one of the pigeons that successfully passed its message on is in a Historic Hangar at the RAF Museum in Hendon, with the inscription 'A Very Gallant Gentleman' under its preserved body.

Inevitably the increased use of aircraft in the Second World War prompted the growth of Search and Rescue throughout the Royal Navy, not just as a result of the planes flying back from raids across the Channel, but also because of the number that ditched off the side of carriers. The first recorded Royal Navy SAR dive took place on 16 April 1944, when the Allies destroyed an oil refinery used by the Japanese on an island off the north coast of Sumatra. When one of the returning

Grumman Hellcat fighters that had launched from the carrier USS *Saratoga* ditched into the sea, the submarine HMS *Tactician*, which had accompanied the battle fleet, acted swiftly. The submarine's commander sent his two best swimmers, Petty Officer Leading Torpedo Operator Iain Nethercott and Leading Stoker Frank Mustard, into the water to see what they could do to rescue the pilot, whose plane was starting to sink. By the time they had reached the site, after swimming over from the submarine, the plane was already ten feet down and sinking fast. The two men swam down to the plane and saw that the American pilot seemed to be okay inside – there was a bubble of air about his head – but the canopy was jammed. The plane carried on drifting slowly into the darkness below while the two men tore at the canopy when, as the Hellcat neared twenty feet, Frank Mustard found the emergency release lever and together the two British sailors pulled on it. The canopy lifted and fell away, and they dragged the pilot out, by which time the plane had drifted to thirty feet down. Lungs bursting, the two British sailors pulled the American up with them as his plane sank into the deep, and dragged themselves on to the deck of *Tactician*. The Americans awarded the commander of the submarine a medal for this rescue.

Another incident marked the development of a fully fledged SAR Diver's programme, although it doesn't have a happy ending at all. A Navy pilot, Commander Russell, drowned when his Scimitar went over the side of HMS *Victorious* in the English Channel, just off Portsmouth, in 1958. Although rescuers did manage to reach his plane, Cdr Russell remained trapped inside and went down with his aircraft. The incident, coming as it did when *Victorious* was just about to re-enter service after a lengthy and costly refit, was widely publicized, and it was this publicity that led to changes in the way that SAR tasks were thought of in the Navy. A third of all deaths in the Fleet Air Arm from 1955 to 1961 were as a result of aircraft ditching at sea, so after 1961 not only was proper diving equipment made available to aircrews, but Aircrewmen started to be trained as divers too.

771 Naval Air Squadron started life in May 1939 as a 'Fleet Requirements Unit', a support squadron. At the end of the war, the first helicopters – Hoverflies, so explaining the three hoverflies on the squadron's badge – joined the squadron; however, it was disbanded in the mid-1950s. The Navy never mothballs any squadron for ever, though, and 771 was re-formed in 1961; now equipped with Dragonflies, Whirlwinds and the Wasp prototype, the squadron was based at RNAS Portland and tasked with helicopter trials and training roles. 771 pioneered many techniques now commonplace in SAR, such as free-diver drops and developing cliff-rescue techniques. In 1974 the squadron was subdivided into 772 Squadron at Portland and 771 Squadron at RNAS Culdrose, where it continued its role as a training squadron, with a dedicated SAR flight. Five

years later 771's SAR flight was upgraded with the change to Wessex Mk 5 aircraft. Since the late 1980s 771 has flown Westland Sea Kings, a variation, built under licence, of the US Sikorsky S-61 helicopter. The range the new helicopter gave 771 meant that its operational area covered the whole of Devon and Cornwall and the surrounding sea, the Isles of Scilly, the Western Channel and up to 200 nautical miles from the coast.

771 is a slightly unusual squadron in that everyone who is in the squadron has applied to be there; it is normal Royal Navy practice to rotate personnel into the section where they're needed, but 771 is unusual as the one squadron that is staffed by people who have specifically applied to go into the SAR world with the Navy. There are about 200 people on the squadron in total; however, on any given day, there are likely to be fewer than half that number actually on duty. That's twenty-eight officers, the pilots and Observers, and ten Aircrewmen, together with an additional group of pilots, Observers and Aircrewmen, made up of some Royal Navy Reserves, maybe a Junglie (someone from one of the Commando squadrons) or two, or someone seconded to the squadron. We often have pilots from the US, from the RAF or from other NATO forces with us. The Aircrewmen are non-commissioned and will have completed tours on Anti-Submarine/Anti-Surface Warfare (ASW) or one of the Commando squadrons, prior to completing the specialist SAR course to introduce them to the new role before

becoming full-time members of the crew. 771's engineering section consists of three officers, with about 140 Senior and Junior Rates, with a few RNR Rates as well. The engineers – and I should know, having been one, though not for 771 but earlier when working in a Commando role – perform amazing miracles with the Sea Kings, working night and day in watches to keep the aircraft flying.

Working in the Commando role meant being in a stripped-down Sea King, with no radar (although some have cameras now), mostly acting as a troop carrier out on operations in places like Iraq and Afghanistan. They carry out troop evacuations, heavy load moves, amphibious operations, inserts, all sorts of things. Out at sea the Commando Sea Kings operate from different types of ships to us, and because the Marines wear camouflage uniforms we refer to them, and their aircraft, as the Junglies.

771 began its time at Culdrose on one side of the airfield, away from the main buildings; the SAR element of the job was much smaller than now, when it's the main task the squadron performs; back then it was managed solely as a flight, that is, with no more than two or three aircraft. Now, it's in a central position on HMS *Seahawk* – the Royal Navy's name for the base at Culdrose – and the SAR aspect of the squadron's work has become a defining part of 771's role within the Navy.

A major change since those days is the shift of power

within the squadron away from the Aircrewmen, who used to run it, towards the Observers – who are officers. The Aircrewmen were led by the SAR Divers, who were the specialists, capable of surface or sub-surface swimming; that's why they considered themselves important. When the squadron moved, the Observers started to play a much greater role. The boss then was an Observer and a new position of Senior Observer was created. There are now as many Observers as there are crewmen. The Aircrewmen became the ones who went up and down on the winch and the Observer took over the role of handling the winch while the crewman was outside the aircraft. The Observer is not always the aircraft captain (the current boss of the squadron is a pilot), because in the aircraft seniority doesn't always count – more frequently it's experience that matters. Quite often the pilot and Observer will turn to someone like Dave Rigg – who has been on the squadron longer than anybody else – as he has done a lot more jobs than either of them: 'Dave, can we do this job?' And there have been occasions where the crewmen have known that something can be achieved that the less experienced but more senior men on board can't do. Dave has told me about times when, 'I've been on jobs where the Observer's looked and said, "I can't put you on there"; and I've said, "Fine, get your double-lift harness on, I can put you on. Get down there, you're not going to like much, but I can get you down there!"' With the bringing together of the aircraft commander's role with that of the Observer, the balance within the helicopter changed and the personnel on board the Sea King went from a five-man to a four-man crew.

The work of 771 started to expand beyond the military world during the 1970s, and while the squadron has always undertaken this kind of bread-and-butter work, and some people like to think of taking injured sailors off fishing trawlers and other boats that way, it was the big disasters that received national publicity which made the difference to the way 771 was thought of not only in the public eye but also within the SAR world – and the Royal Navy. Getting known for lifting injured men off trawlers had its drawbacks: we used to attend trawlers out at sea regularly, to take off a fisherman who had been complaining of chest pains . . . only for him to then make a rapid, almost miraculous recovery. We'd risk life and limb to get out there and get him in, only for the doctors to find a perfect heart trace – there was nothing wrong with him. Or someone would be reported with 'severe abdominal pains': we would worry about what medical kit we were going to need, we'd fly out there and when we were about to be put down we'd find them standing on the deck waving up at us cheerfully, bags packed and ready to go. There was a spate of it a few years ago. It was mostly Spanish fishermen, who would be taken on for two-month-long sea-tours, some of them young lads who then realized they didn't really want to be on a boat any longer.

It's much more common for the squadron, though, to be facing real problems, real catastrophes. The combination of sea and bad weather can be lethal, and disasters can happen all too easily. Probably the most well-known disaster off the Cornish coast that 771 Squadron was involved in was the Fastnet race in 1979, the 'worst disaster in the one hundred years of ocean yacht racing' it's been called. Fifteen people died: six men were swept overboard and lost at sea, while nine others either drowned or died of hypothermia. The race started in relatively calm conditions but the weather soon deteriorated into a Force 11 storm, and over the next few days twenty-four crews abandoned their yachts, five of which sank. The Royal Navy coordinated the rescue and helicopters from RNAS Culdrose flew a total of sixty-two sorties, over 195 hours in all, bringing in seventy-four men and women who had to be rescued. They also had the sad task of collecting and returning two of the bodies. The rest of the crews, who had either abandoned ship or been taken off their yachts, were brought in by lifeboat, their fellow sailors, or by commercial or naval seamen.

Fastnet, over the years, continued to be a race in which people would get into difficulties. During the 1985 race the yacht *Drum*, crewed by among others Simon LeBon from Duran Duran, capsized and left several of the crew trapped under the hull. 771 again rescued them, the SAR Diver on the crew – Larry Slater – diving under the water and up into the hull space to free them. Maybe because there was a pop star on board this rescue got a lot of coverage, and, unlikely as it sounds, Larry even made it to the heights of fame, appearing on *This is Your Life* a year later.

Sadly, the crews could do little to avoid the terrible loss of life on 19 December 1981, when the Penlee life-boat disappeared as it tried to rescue the crew and passengers of the *Union Star*. The *Union Star* fell into difficulties after developing an engine fault off the south coast of Cornwall; she was being driven on to the rocks of Boscawen Cove, and so put out a distress signal to the Falmouth Coastguard. The conditions were so appalling, with the winds gusting up over 85 knots, that the Sea King – not one from 771 on this occasion but from 820 NAS, which was then ashore at Culdrose – was unable to remove any of the five crew and three passengers – the Captain's wife and stepdaughters – on board. The helicopter record, written by the Captain, an American on an exchange visit, Lieutenant Commander Russell Smith, stated: 'Attempted three normal double-lift transfers. Wind velocity/sea state/ship movement/aircraft movement made this method impossible. Aircraft was between 120/60ft. Attempted six high-line transfers.'

Meanwhile the lifeboat from the Cornish village of Mousehole, the *Solomon Browne*, with its experienced crew of eight volunteers, launched at Penlee Point. The crew had been chosen carefully, with only one man from each family allowed to get into the lifeboat.

49

Lieutenant Commander Smith continued to find the behaviour of those on board the *Union Star* puzzling, given the terrible nature of the storm around them: 'Aside from a ship's crewman putting ladder over side, no persons came out of bridge except to occasionally open port door and wave at RNLI crew who had been gesturing to come out since arriving on scene. There seemed no sense of urgency from Ship's crew.'

Time was running out for the helicopter, as it was burning tremendous amounts of fuel against the gusting winds in order to stay on scene. The crew continued to try and get a line down to the ship, even when discussions had moved from trying to launch the ship's life raft to planning to jump into the lifeboat coming alongside – which was being hammered against the *Union Star* by the waves as a result of this manoeuvre. 'On three occasions,' noted Lieutenant Commander Smith, 'line dragged across deck within 3–4 feet of ship's crewman. No attempt was made to chase after the line.'

In mountainous seas, where the waves reached over sixty feet, the *Solomon Browne* had managed to get some of the passengers and crew from *Union Star* on board but went back to recover the rest, and was never seen again. Other lifeboats tried to join in the rescue, and the search was also joined by helicopters from RNAS Culdrose, but the visibility and turbulence had worsened since earlier in the evening and Lieutenant Commander Smith noted: 'Accurate search flying impossible in the conditions.' Both vessels were lost, with all sixteen on board losing their lives; eight bodies were eventually recovered, four from the eight-man crew of the lifeboat and four from the *Union Star*.

Why had things gone so badly wrong on this rescue? There had been a question of salvage rights to the *Union Star* which slowed up the initial sending out of the distress call – that type of thing needed to be sorted out, and was. There was, however, only one proper response to such an event, which was for us to train and train and perfect techniques to make sure such a thing will never happen again. The organizations that give us our orders, too, have to review how they respond to distress calls of this nature, and while of course some things can never be planned for, other elements can be changed. A disaster such as that affects the entire SAR world and the lifeboat organization as a whole, but obviously devastates a community like Mousehole.

The Penlee lifeboat disaster showed only too clearly how vital a role 771 has to play in Search and Rescue; and how, even with the best training and equipment, and the most committed and fearless of personnel, the sea can still prove murderous.

# 3. WAFU to SAR Diver

It was four years later before I was able to switch branches – it's a lot faster now – so in 1997 I marched on to HMS *Seahawk*, better known as Royal Naval Air Station Culdrose. Once notice finally came through that they were ready for me, there was a two-day medical pulling me apart, before they measured me for my flying overalls. They ran a measure over every bit of me, my reach from fingertips to toes, in all sorts of different postures – sitting, standing, reaching – and then comically I'm handed an off-the-shelf pair of overalls anyway. Perhaps I'm just the right size for their kit – or maybe it was a case of any size you like as long as it's medium.

One of the reasons I had to wait before I could switch branches was that I had to be able to tick all the boxes I needed for the job. First up was a Leading Rates' Command course, which took place over three weeks at Whales Island and which I didn't like at all: lots of physical stuff and a lot of charging about. So I wasn't looking forward to the next course, the Senior Leading Rates' Command course. This took four weeks and although it was physically hard work again, with the added difficulty of learning the skills necessary to be a proper team leader, it turned out to be a lot better than the Leading Rates' course, and much more competitive too – I thought it was absolutely brilliant. Next I had to go through a grading exercise, a further two weeks (only this time at Culdrose) of taking part in loads of basic exams, some of which consisted of computer-based multiple-choice answering, in different fields. There was some basic acoustic tracking, to see if I could get my head round Doppler Theory and then some hands-on sonar tracking of submarines, learning the difference between false contacts and actual under-water craft. I did those tests in an office in front of a computer, while now it's a bit more state of the art as it's done in a Sea King simulator.

Once I'd started in the aircrew world at Culdrose, I kept my ears open all the time, as I wanted to learn everything I could about the Aircrewman's role in Search and Rescue in the time I had available. I started to hear more about the other aspects of the job, and one in particular – diving – really appealed to me. On the Aircrewman's course before and alongside mine there were a few lads, Nobby Hall, Andy Penrose and Bomber, who talked about trying out for SAR Divers – they were all already Ship's Divers. I listened to them and the more I heard the more I fancied diving; even if only half of what they said turned out to be true it still sounded really cool: jumping out of aircraft, winching people up to safety – that was an exciting idea.

'I'm going to do that Ship's Diver's course,' I declared

one day, egged on by the others; but even then in the back of my mind was the thought that if it went well I'd have a go at the SAR diving course too. As we progressed through the course, Nobby became more determined to be a SAR Diver and echoed my thought when he told me: 'I joined the branch for this, this is what I want to do.' I thought hard about doing the Ship's Diver's course, knowing how tough it would be, but I also knew that it would turn me from never-dived-before into a fully qualified diver in an intense few weeks. I understood that to mean I'd be day-diving all day long, and then on Tuesdays and Thursdays I'd be night-diving as well. There would be no time for anything else. I'd finish my diving for the morning, then run round to change, straight into the mess to eat whatever was put in front of me double-quick time, run back, sit down, have a couple of lessons – and I guessed that what we would learn in the classroom would be hard, because everything I'd heard from the other lads told me this was no easy part of the course – then straight back in the water for the rest of the afternoon and dive again. I would be knackered all the time, but I'd be achieving something that I really wanted.

If only I'd known; the Ship's Diver's course, which if I wanted to become a SAR Diver was a prerequisite, was a hellish four weeks of near-constant diving in an inland saltwater lake at Horsea Island in Portsmouth. Except of course my vision of hell usually involved flames and heat; the water in the lake at Horsea Island is permanently just above freezing – it's nine metres deep most of the way round, so the cold seems to grow out of the bottom of the lake to prevent the water ever warming up – so it was very, very unpleasant to jump into, no matter what kit I was wearing. There is negligible visibility, as most of that nine metres is silt, which, once stirred up, rises to block any light. It's a big lake, origin-ally built for torpedo trials, about three quarters of a mile long and a hundred yards wide, and I know to my cost what it's like to try running round that distance in full kit with twin cylinders on my back, when I'd already emerged from the water exhausted.

The course itself was quite harsh, with a lot of phys-ical exercise, the worst of which were the mud runs, where those of us foolish enough to do the course were expected to run through the knee- and hip-deep mud in the bay in our dive suits. All of us were expected to be able to take whatever grim tasks we were set and do them all at top speed, even if already exhausted by the time they started; this was after all a military course and the examiners expected us to reach minimum levels to enable us to do the job.

Having been a WAFU – a Weapons and Fuel User – all my working life, I was now in a completely alien environment. I was in the world of diving and was treated worse than a new recruit – about the politest thing said of all us trainee divers was when we were referred to as a 'Ship's Blip'. The instructors were the Clearance Divers, the professional divers in the Navy, responsible for among other things clearing mines and other munitions away from the Royal Navy's ships, and they'd excelled in the Falklands in 1982, working with the warships and harbours in the cold South Atlantic water. As far as my instructors were concerned I was something smelly they'd stepped in, and if I couldn't take their beasting then I was of no use to them or to the branch. But it made a few of us on the course good divers. It's a three-week course, turning a student from someone who has never dived before to someone familiar with diving under a ship, which – the first time I did it anyway – is a horrific experience.

Some people might have done the Ship's Diver's course just for the extra £3.50 a day, but I thought they were mad if that was their only reason for doing it – you'd have to enjoy it, if only a little bit, simply because of the type of diving we were expected to do. It was very claustrophobic, even quite scary at times, especially when some of our equipment could get wrapped round a prop or something because there's no one there to help us; there's someone else on the end of the line but if I can hardly see the prop or the A-frame I've managed to get wrapped up in, they can't help pull me out. If I'd only ever done the course with the aim of remaining in that area, after what I came to find out about what's involved with clearance diving, I don't think I would have completed the course to be honest. It was, at times, truly horrible.

A lot of the exercises on the course were designed to

build up our stamina and test our resolve. On our first day, the instructors set about demonstrating to us novices how they were going to go about doing this – we had to swim with all our kit on to the end of the lake, where we had to ring a bell before we could swim back. Naturally it wasn't as simple as stretching an arm out of the water to ring the bell – we had to clamber out of the water in our dive kit and hoist ourselves over a little ridge to reach it. This was after a fifty- to sixty-minute swim to get to the end. Of course, we were told: 'When you get there and you've rung the bell, we'll drive down and give you a lift back' – do they heck. We had to take our fins off and run back in full kit – but at least it was the short way back, directly to the centre, rather than all the way round the other side of the lake and back again. The first time I did this, I was no good at all, as one of the things this exercise is designed to teach is not that I didn't have the capacity for the course but how to breathe underwater so as to prolong the air in my cylinders and so extend the amount of time I could spend underwater, even when exerting myself – it was easier to swim underwater as I wasn't fighting against the surface tension and the waves. When I first did the swim I emerged at some point halfway along the lake, gasping, and I wasn't allowed simply to swim to the side and go back to the dive centre the short way round – oh no. I had to swim to the opposite bank and then run – in my full kit – the long way back to the centre.

When I arrived back at the diving dock I immediately had to change my kit then get straight back in the water again. We novices were never, ever, allowed a moment's rest. But it was good because it did dramatically change my fitness levels as I didn't stop, and I trained myself to get to the end of everything with some energy to spare. Just as well, really, because the end never came.

Like most people who take up diving, I had no idea what being under water would be like – not what the underwater world would be like but what the experience of being underwater would be like for me. How would I cope physically? Would I manage well with what is, after all, an alien environment? In the end I was surprised at how easy I found the transition from air to water to be. I was no different to anyone learning to dive who has difficulty, at first, in controlling their breathing so that they can spend longer times under water. The only difference for me was the experience of swimming down Horsea Lake, only to realize I was running out of air and knowing that I didn't dare risk coming up to the surface because of the bellowing I'd receive from the instructors. In the end I learned to inhale and exhale as two separate parts of the same action, like a pendulum swinging from one side to another, with a small gap in between, so that I could prolong my time underwater.

When we were taken elsewhere for diving, it was to dive under ships in Portsmouth Harbour. The ship we used mostly was HMS *Bristol*, a Type 82 destroyer that was primarily employed at that time for Sea Cadet training and was tied up alongside Whale Island. HMS *Bristol* was big, large enough to throw a deep shadow, so it was very gloomy under her. She no longer moved and had no propeller any more, and around the bottom of the ship a layer of fine silt had built up. The layer was deep enough, when the tide went out, for a diver to squeeze in quite close between the keel and the bottom – it was like a muddy sink, and pitch black under there even on a sunny day. Of course, we trainees were not allowed torches or gloves, because we were on a course and as Ship's Blips we had to put up with this. At night it was impossible to see anything; normally for a diver the simplest way of knowing the essential fact of which way is up, back to the surface and air, is by watching which way the bubbles rise – even if you're disoriented, you know that bubbles are going to go up, so you follow them to the surface. Of course, in the dark under HMS *Bristol* we couldn't even see the bubbles, and that was pretty frightening. What we learned to do was to take a Cyalume – one of those fluorescent tubes you snap to release a chemical light – under our masks, right beside our eyes, which gave us about an inch of visibility. Worse still, as I peered out over the green glow from the Cyalume, was that there were these . . . things . . . reaching out to you from the dark. Because she doesn't move anywhere now, HMS *Bristol* has become home to what are known as 'dead man's fingers', which grow all the way along the keel; it's a form of kelp which grows in big white tubes. They're skeletal-like and hang there and just brush a diver's head swimming past them – what a horrible feeling it was to see these fingers loom out of the dark at the very last moment, almost as if they were reaching out to stroke my hair. I'd grit my teeth and carry on. The only way I survived that course was through pure determination – I am going to get through this – because you know what the instructors are aiming to do: they're trying to weed out the weak.

The final straw for many on the course was when we were night-diving on the *Liverpool*, which is an operational ship because we have to go and dive 'live' ships in harbour. For dives such as this, we would group together in what was called a necklace; one of the course instructors would take a line and swim with it on the surface along one side of the ship and round the other, and then us novices would hold on to this line, positioned at intervals all the way down the ship to the keel and back. It was a method used by Royal Navy divers checking the hull of a ship for any damage or anything left there by other divers, such as explosives. But the sides of the ship are not featureless and smooth; there are all sorts of things on operational ships such as an impeller (which is like a propeller, except that it is in a tube which sucks water through and jets it out). There was a curious low-pitched hum around the ship – probably the metal reflecting the sounds coming through the water made by other activity in the harbour. It was of course dark, and naturally we were still not allowed torches. The obvious problem of a group dive like this is that once the line has gone round the back end, the line of divers shifts on to different levels around the hull. It's impossible for it not to, not least because novice divers like my group were not all of the same ability – some of us had only started diving a week and a half before, for the first time ever, and in the dark we had to watch out for the clutter at the back of the keel. There were two rudders and two props, at different heights and surrounded by A-frames, and that's where the accident occurred.

The instructors had us going down in groups, and after one group had come up another team would be sent down. When they pointed to me, telling me to get my kit on again, I felt I'd had enough; I was beyond freezing, actually shaking uncontrollably at that point. 'No damn way,' I said, surprising myself. 'I've already dived twice, straight after each other, I'm totally freezing and there's people here that haven't dived yet.'

I could have been done for insubordination but instead all that came back was 'Oh, all right.' Another diver was picked and off they went; and on the team that went down one guy became stuck under the back of the keel. Unfortunately he panicked, and ripped his mask off underwater. The dive was abandoned and the necklace brought to the surface. As for the guy taken out, that was the end of him on the course, but he wasn't alone. What had happened had freaked some of the other divers out. I watched as they came back to the surface and as soon as three of the guys climbed back to the boat, they said, 'That's it, I'm off the course now, this is just rubbish, you can keep your £3.50 extra.'

Those of us left turned up the next day and went through some more grief, namely the replacement for the mud runs – abandoned on account of their being dangerous, we were told. We had to swim ashore from the boat in our dry suits and fins, then get our fins off and – what's this? Mud? We had to run through mud above our knees to a can buoy which was about 300 yards away and get back – that was knackering. All the time we were being screamed at from start to finish, to get back in the water to fin across about 100 yards to a platform, a painting platform alongside HMS *Scylla* (she was waiting for disposal and is now off Whitsun Bay as a dive wreck). When we reached the platform we had to climb up through the ship to the top, get to the bridge wing, take one look down – *damn,* that's high up – and jump, get our fins back on when we were in the water and swim back round the can buoy to do it all over again, until we would start falling over. The aim of it, so we were told, was to instil high levels of fitness and endurance in us, both a big part of the kind of diving we were going to do – as well as getting us used to jumping off a high platform. Mostly I thought it was through sheer bloody-mindedness – the old 'we did this, so you have to too' factor.

I wasn't going to be beaten, so I passed the course and qualified as a Ship's Diver, and was able to move on to my next goal – to become an SAR Diver.

The object of the Ship's Diver's course is to turn a non-diver into a qualified diver within the shortest possible time. The object of the SAR Diver's course was to put the applicant – me – through the worst possible pressures they could expect to face – involving heights, dark and tight spaces, exhaustion and fear. The SAR Diver's training was designed to turn a diver into one of the most highly trained specialist ratings in the Royal Navy. As with other Navy divers, the SAR Diver was cleared to work down to a depth of thirty metres, but the unique feature of his working life was that, unlike any other diver in the Navy, he was able to detach himself from any line to a boat or aircraft and swim freely to conduct his rescue. Being able to detach from a cable and swim with no lifeline or indeed any physical link to the ship gave the SAR Diver freedom but also the responsibility to carry out his tasks without jeopardizing his own safety or that of others.

SAR Divers were volunteers who had completed at least one front-line tour as an ASW Aircrewman and clocked up at least 500 minutes' underwater time *after* qualifying as a Ship's Diver. When I'd completed the Ship's Diver's course, I returned to Culdrose and started working as a member of staff in the diving centre, assisting the instructors on the SAR course, helping my mate Nobby get through it. Thanks to this situation, I had met the 'minutes underwater' requirement when I came to start my SAR Diver's course.

Working with Nobby on his SAR Diver's course was very useful to me, but I like to think I helped him pass it, because he struggled. He had a bit of an injury to his ankle and his wife kept on at him to pull out before the injury got worse or he damaged something else. I said, 'No way, mate, you've come this far, your whole life's going to change, you want to do this.' Selfishly, of course, because I wanted to do it myself, so I pushed and pulled him to go through with it and I'm glad to say he finished it successfully. It certainly paid off for me, that time helping Nobby, as I learned a lot. It was a good introduction to 771 and over the three months we were flying we went on some great training missions. I became keener than I had ever been on taking on this role for myself.

If I'd thought the Ship's Diver's course was bad, the SAR Diver's course was a lot, lot worse. Because we were doing so many dives a day I was beating my body up on a daily basis, popping pills just to get through it – horse-size tablets of ibuprofen, decongestants, ear sprays, eye sprays – I was in and out of the water so much I was trying to fend off all sorts of bugs. I was doing all sorts of stuff just to keep myself going. Towards the end of the course I was absolutely knackered, it was about nine o'clock at night – in other words we'd had an early finish – and I thought I'd treat myself and have a Guinness. I went down to the local pub, where the woman behind the bar knew me. She took one searching look at me and said, 'You all right? I've not seen you for ages. You look really, really, ill.'

I looked gaunt and white, not having seen much daylight as I was either in the water, in the aircraft or in the classroom. I was also very thin, because I'd lost between a stone and a half and two stone in weight, even though I was eating like a pig. 'No, I'm okay, I'm not ill, I've just been on a diving course.'

'Oh, thank God for that, I thought with not seeing you recently and you looking like that you had cancer.' Nice. Thanks.

By the time I was ready to do my SAR Diver's course, not only did I know a lot about what was going to happen, but I also knew a lot of the guys who'd successfully completed it – Nobby Hall, Julian 'Bungi' Williams, Andy Penrose, Alex Stevenson. I knew what they'd been through, and how hard it had been for them to complete the course. If I was ever going to be ready for it, now was the time.

The training started at the Dive School, at 6.30 a.m. on Monday, which I knew meant that we – John Smith and Ryan 'Nic' Nicholls, the two others on the course, and myself – had to be there and ready to go at 6 a.m. The rest of the time went like that; whatever start time we were given – say, 6.30 a.m. at Falmouth quayside – was the time they expected us to be there, kitted up and ready to get in the water, everything prepared for the day ahead. There was no swanning in at 6.35 a.m., coffee in hand – I'd have been binned immediately if I'd done that. The first day started with some admin work, where the diver running the course introduced himself:

'I'm Steve Bielby, I'm the Chief Diver. You are here to try and pass the toughest course of your life. Your course will last four weeks, and you will live in the Transit van for most of those four weeks. When you're not in the van, you'll be diving or running. There are no exceptions to this. You will spend these weeks jumping in the water, off the harbour, off aircraft, and conducting exercises under the water. The next few weeks will be endless days of dive after dive after dive; there will be a lot of PT to make sure you are all fit for this. You will be expected to pass surface and sub-surface endurance swims. You will train to recover panicky surface swimmers, as well as rescuing unconscious divers from the seabed. When I am satisfied with your progress, and not before, we will go to Horsea Island and you will dive there to rescue bodies from ambulances and other vehicles submerged in the water. If you pass that part of the course, then we will go to the Dunker and you will train there, in the dark, with and without a mask. If I feel you are ready at that point then you will pass the course. Any questions?'

Silence. We knew all this already – despite the fact this was supposed to be the first day of the course, Steve had already had us doing some aptitude tests the week before.

The aptitude tests hadn't been too bad, some standard fitness work, that sort of thing. We'd also had to do some diving in the pool at Culdrose, to satisfy Steve we were at a minimum level – even though we'd all clocked up hours and hours underwater, he wanted to be sure himself. When he'd been running a Clearance Diver's course elsewhere there'd been some accidents and he really didn't want anything to go wrong on this course, not when his retirement was looming. So he made us go through some basics, like checking we could go down in zero visibility, flood our face masks, which are not like ones snorkellers wear but full-face masks, as we weren't qualified on BASAR (Breathing Apparatus. Air Search and Rescue) in Steve's eyes, even if we'd dived before, until he said so. For the test we had to dive to the bottom of the pool, lift the seal of the mask from around our faces to flood our masks, return to the surface to show him we'd flooded it, go back down, clear the mask of water, come back up and show him that we'd successfully emptied the mask and had full vision again. That's a fairly standard part of any diver's training to be honest, it doesn't take long to learn, but it does freak a lot of people out, especially when they first try it in the open ocean rather than a pool. It was easier in the old days with the full-face mask because the breathing tube was separate, and we could carry on breathing even with water inside the mask; now we can't, and we have to hold our breath while flooding our masks, but it's still not hard. The other tests were

67

things like companion-dive drills, surfacing drills, buddy-breathing underwater.

Steve's aptitude test, which he'd designed himself, also had an exam element to it. He wanted to see if you had mastered things like underwater signals – what you have to make use of if the communications fail – which is a series of pulls and bells, controlled by a rope. You had to pass with 100 per cent on that, and 80 per cent on everything else, which was everything from explaining diving disorders and diseases to demonstrating the companion-dive routine or surfacing drill. The three of us – John, Nic and myself – had coped with all this, and had at least made it to the opening day of the course. Nic and John were both in their mid-thirties; Nic was an ASW crewman who had come through the same route as me, although he had more diving experience because he had worked in the Dunker, so he was Survival Equipment rated as well. John had done his Ship's Diver's course and had enough minutes to qualify as a SAR Diver; he was at the other end of the spectrum in terms of diving experience. He was a Royal Marine, so he had a background as a Commando crewman, and he'd come down to Culdrose for a tour on 771. During that time he decided to become a SAR Diver, so he got his minutes in and just fitted the criteria. It meant a lot of work for him as, like me, he had had to do the Ship's Diver's course first.

'Good,' Steve continued. He then introduced the

other instructors on the course, most of whom I knew already: Andy Penrose, Alex Stevenson, 'Whisky' Walker (who now runs the Dunker), Ben Daddow and Des Hammond.

Steve continued: 'I want you to read and sign these forms. When you've signed them then we'll do some PT, after which we will go through the layout of the kit rooms, and you can draw your kit for the weeks ahead.' The forms were all to do with safety. Steve explained his thinking behind the way he was going to teach us on the course, and how he felt that it was when we were diving that we were most in danger – not when we were getting in and out of the water:

'If you're going to die, chances are it'll be under the water, not getting down to it; you're going to die under the water because there's no way anybody can see you, apart from the bubbles coming up, if you're lucky, there'll be no other visible sign of you. As a SAR Diver, you are completely self-supervisory, you're not tethered to anybody, everything relies on your wits and training. As you know, this is the opposite ethos to sport and military diving, which says you will dive with a buddy, that you'll not be more than a metre and a half apart, that you'll be tethered and constantly checking on each other. What I'm going to teach you is the other end of the spectrum – you'll learn to jump out of that aircraft and be totally, completely on your own. Questions?'

The silence grew a little deeper.

'Good. Now get your sports kit on and let's get started.' And off we went on our BFT – a Battle Fitness Test. We had to run a mile and a half warm-up within fifteen minutes, followed by a mile and a half in under ten and a half minutes, followed by sixteen dips, sixteen push-ups, sixteen burpees, eight chin-to-bar pull-ups (the hard ones), and loads of other stuff designed to test us. Again, having been on Nobby's course, I'd known this was coming so we three had done a couple of weeks working up to it, fitness-wise; we'd do some running daily around the base – there's a route opposite called the Triangle, which we ran regularly.

Once we were done with the BFT, it was back to the Dive School for a shower, get changed and get into drawing our kit. We had to draw a lot of kit as well, from the collection of dive sets hanging on the wall. There were over twenty in various stages of use; we didn't get our own dive sets but the pre-use and post-use checks were second to none, mostly because we were taught to go through every item meticulously ourselves – it was our own safety we were checking, after all. We were issued our own wetsuit, which was the old-style one until we passed and only then would we be considered ready to wear the SAR Diver's stand-ard red suit. All except me, that is. I'd put myself forward to try out a new-style wetsuit while on the course. The Navy was changing the contract for the supply of divers' suits and was going to have one con-tract for all the Navy's divers, so I had 'volunteered' to try a few things out for them. The suit I was issued was thinner, and therefore more flexible, and supposedly just as thermally protected as the old suits. However, as soon as I took it out I could see it was awful – cheap and nasty – it looked like it had been glued together with paper glue. Andy Penrose picked it up and rubbed the material between his fingers, before declaring: 'I couldn't dive in that thing, it's horrible.' It took me about ten seconds in the open water to discover I agreed with him. It was about as protective as going in naked – I've never been so cold in my life, and I was left shuddering through every dive, all the way through the day, thinking, 'I. AM. NOT. ENJOYING. THIS.' The suit quickly became known to all of us on the course as the discount wetsuit, because it seemed like the kind of item you'd find on the shelves of a discount store in Falmouth. I put up with the suit for as long as I could before binning it after the trip to Horsea Island, where it was 4°C and I had to be helped out of the suit afterwards because I was so stiff with cold I couldn't move my fingers.

Normal service on the course would mean showing up at the Dive School at about 0600, getting our kit into the van and be down in Falmouth with our suits on in fast order. The three of us would have to be dressed in a few seconds, in the freezing cold even though we were inside the van. It was February; it was unbelievably awful getting naked in the back of a Transit van when it was still dark outside. We'd rigged a load of wires up in the back of the van to act as a sort of drying rack, with wet kit hanging in there, so we'd just have to get cold and get on with it, knowing we'd warm up shortly, especially at the start of the day. First thing we'd be sent up the giraffe, where we'd do our quick checks – time, check; compass, check; gloves, check – in a second, and then jump off the top platform into the cold water thirty or so feet below – the height varied depending on how highly inflated the giraffe was. The first lesson we learned was that if the surface of the water was untroubled and still it was like hitting glass at that time of the morning, so we didn't jump from a greater height till the surface was disturbed. We worked out a few years ago that the surface tension of the water – because it's flat there in the sheltered areas – is far greater than when we're jumping from an aircraft, so it really does makes a difference. It hurt a lot more, because the impact wore me down after I'd done ten of those. Off I'd go, swim back up to the surface and across to the steps on the other side of the quay, at full belt on my back, just finning, out on to the quayside, up the steps as fast as I could, run round, get my fins back on, and stand behind Nic or John, whoever was in front, shout out my time, back up to the top, off I'd go again. Ten of those, and that was just to warm up. Once we were done Steve Bielby would shout out: 'Right, get dressed, we're going for a navigation dive.'

That sounds simple enough but of course it never was. We were always cold, so that we couldn't handle zips and fasteners easily, and as we had a mountain of kit in the back of the van, there were always obstacles to negotiate as we slid out of one sodden outfit and into the next. We carried all this kit so as to be sure we had enough for the two roles a SAR Diver would expect to face: that is, surface and sub-surface; sub-surface kit is the same without, obviously, the yellow inflatable life-jacket. The dive sets themselves were charged by a generator we kept in a Portacabin on the quayside; we'd have three sets for us, and another three sets for the next dive, and a spare set in case one went wrong. One of the assistant instructors in the boat had a set on standby, ready for immediate use in case there was a problem. All that takes up room in the boat, along with the five of us in there; this equipment took a real battering because it was in use so much. Later on, as we got through the first couple of days, we went on to fully weighted jumps, where we wore a weight belt plus a dive set made up of two inverted five-litre air cylinders on our backs, plus all the rest of the kit, and we're training to throw ourselves out of an aircraft with all this weight on us at around forty feet. Put it this way – most divers, military or otherwise, will jump off the back of a boat, which even in the sorts of heavy swell dive boats can go out in doesn't really get to more than a jumping height of ten, maybe twelve feet. Now here I was, getting ready to jump out of a moving aircraft at a height equivalent to three double-decker buses piled on top of one another.

I've never been great with heights. When we were kids, my brother used to throw himself off the bridge at home when the tide was flooding, do a double somer-sault and land on his back or his belly in the water. I had to do the same – I couldn't let him do what I didn't – but I had to push myself to jump off the bridge. Fear of heights is my one major weakness – and the first time I went to the edge of the helicopter and looked down was not something I was looking forward to, even though I was more than comfortable flying. By the time our first jump came, I'd done two weeks of non-stop jumps from the giraffe – at least it felt like that – so that many of the routines came naturally. We'd check each other's kit, but even then I'd run though my own checks, everything on in the right order, straps and catches and buckles all done up as tightly as possible. We'd then take it in turns to shuffle in our fins to the edge of the cab. I was very apprehensive – it felt like I had snakes in my belly – and I looked forward, as we'd been told to do, because that made sure we kept ourselves in the right angle for entering the water. Of course I couldn't resist a glance down – and the sea seemed twice as far away as I had feared it would. Still – no turning back now – and the slap on the shoulder told me, jump! – so I did.

Fortunately the entry into the water was a lot smoother than I'd expected as the water was aerated by the downwash, breaking up the surface tension, although the greater height I'd just jumped meant I travelled a lot further into the water on my initial plunge than I'd prepared for – at least four metres in all. That first jump out of the way, we were immediately expected to return to the aircraft and jump again. This process is a lot more tiring than by the harbourside as each of us had to wait till the others had jumped before we could be picked up. That meant treading water while we did so. Fine. And then once you were out of the water it was a strain as the dive sets weighed a bit when free of the water where they were neutrally buoyant, so I'd be crunching my abdomina muscles to hold myself in place on the winch and not get tipped over backwards by the weight I was carrying.

We also had to work out our own ways of getting back on board the aircraft. Because we had all our gear on, we were told the best way was to slide in backwards once we'd reached the top of the winch cable; Nick refused, and instead flipped in forwards. I've always gone in the same way, the way we were taught, but I developed one funny habit: no one helping me in was to touch my dive gear. It became the rule for anyone working with me; I just couldn't risk someone tugging me in using a strap, only to watch it snap open – or for someone to pull on the top of one of my air cylinders and undo the valve as I was coming in. These problems could be avoided if no one helped me in; so no one did or ever has done.

Next we moved on to exiting from the helicopter facing forwards, which we needed to be taught in case we had to jump out of the aircraft while it was moving rather than in a stationary hover. We had to jump out and turn into the wind while travelling, even though it would be at a sedate speed of, say, 5 knots forward. We had to jump to avoid the step that protruded from the aircraft, then twist so as to prepare our arms for entry into the water – we had about two seconds, when the helicopter was at forty feet, to accomplish this.

That gap in time – two seconds – was our only way of knowing how high up we were. We weren't supposed to be looking down to gauge the distance – except that we always did, because not one of us trusted the instructors – and we were right not to – one time they decided to get us jumping out at a much greater height, between fifty and sixty feet. I only realized it was this high when I jumped – from the helicopter it had looked high enough but when I was in midair, flailing my arms to try and keep myself straight even though I had the weight of my dive set on my back – it was only then, as the seconds ticked away, that I knew exactly how far I was falling – how high I'd jumped. One one-thousand ... two one-thousand ... three one-thousand ... four one-thousand ... five one-thous – *splash*. I knew there was no way this had been a mistake. I'd asked Andy and Alex to lower the aircraft by pointing my thumb downwards, but they'd smiled and shaken their heads, so once I'd had the two taps on my shoulder – the 'go' signal – I had no choice.

Steve Bielby took a very dim view of this and when

we returned to base he let the two of them know it, long and loudly.

It's easy to die if you fall from that height and you don't enter the water properly, and if you fall when you're not expecting to then you tumble down and that's when everything goes wrong. One case of this was rammed home to us during our training. Steve told us about a time quite a few years back when someone did fall out of the strop at that height. 'The chap had just been rescued and winched up to the door of the helicopter; thank you, my saviours, he said to the men waiting at the door of the cab to pull him in – only he raised his arms in a prayer of thanks and so slipped out of the harness and fell into the sea, lost for good. I'm so glad I wasn't there to see that happen,' added Steve, whose determination to avoid any kind of accident is an attitude I myself have stuck to ever since.

Generally, despite whatever Steve Bielby had said we all ended up jumping out of the aircraft from more than forty feet because the assistant instructors still felt we would all benefit from jumping out at those heights, especially when we were exhausted. John, Nic and I didn't really care: we now knew the worst they could do to us, so we'd throw ourselves out of the aircraft, yelling 'Geronimo!' as we fell – what is it this time? Forty feet, fifty feet? Who cares now? We didn't mind any more, we'd crash into the sea, ow! that hurt, better concentrate a bit more on the next one. I'd barely look down – I would shuffle to the doorway, wait for the two taps on my shoulder and off I'd go.

Steve's aim was to drum into us how to jump in whatever condition we were in, whatever condition the sea was in. Hour after hour, day after day, we became used to jumping out at that height and our endurance levels soared. As well as the repetition of the jumps, Steve had us doing tasks: usually they had positioned the squadron's test dummy, Dead Fred, on the seabed, thirty metres down. We had to fin down, following the bubbles coming up from the darkness – the instructors would have put a dive set on him for realism – until we reached him. The idea was to treat him as if he were a diver, so we'd have to check on his status, on his breathing, while one of the assistant instructors watched. Once we'd ascertained he wasn't breathing we had to take him in an unassisted buoyant lift to the surface, which was never easy as Fred was always – well, a dead weight.

Once the exercises in the water were over, there was still no rest for us. As soon as we were on land, we would have to charge our dive sets, and while we were waiting we'd be sent to run some circuits around the quayside. There was no down-time. Even when sitting to listen to Steve explain how we'd got on and what we had to do next, we were expected to be practising knots at the same time, bends and hitches and bowlines. The longest break we had during the day was a ten- or fifteen-minute stop for a sandwich and – if we were lucky – hot soup for lunch. They pushed us hard, all the time. There was no stopping for a rest and we couldn't even be sure what challenge we'd be set next as the instructors planned everything in the boat while we dealt with the current task.

Every morning we started at 6 a.m., dressed and ready to dive, so that meant John, Nic and I had already been to collect our kit and drive it down to the docks before then. We worked twelve-hour days; on Tuesdays and Thursdays, with night-diving, we faced an even longer day. Night-dives were mostly teaching us about navigation, how we had to employ weighted lines to guide us and count the distance we travelled with each fin stroke to know how far we'd gone in one direction before switching to travel in another.

When we'd finished for the day we had to return to the Dive School at Culdrose to clean all the equipment we'd used. It was very important we did this – the double-lift harnesses were really only supposed to be immersed in saltwater once before being refurbished, as otherwise the saltwater would rot them and make them unsafe for lifting people out of the water. We hadn't got the room for that kind of luxury, so every evening the harnesses had to be thoroughly soaked in clean water and then hung up to dry overnight. The drying room at Culdrose did its job but the rest of our gear was hung up in the back of the van, and that meant it was always cold and damp.

Steve made a lot of teaching us how to handle a

panicking swimmer, and we trained for dealing with this first in the pool – to learn the techniques – before moving on to work in the open sea. We would take it in turns to jump off the giraffe in the harbour and approach our swimmer – one of the killick – Leading Seaman – divers when we were training and then one of us once we'd got the idea and were just practising. The way I was taught to deal with it involved my BCD, the Buoyancy Control Device, which is a vest-like item we'd wear over our suits. I'd approach the panicking person while beneath the water, swimming till I was almost immediately under him, then start to inflate my BCD so that I would pop out of the water a bit like a torpedo. As I rose alongside the swimmer I would grip him firmly, bringing him up out of the water with me as I went up, so as to give him a sense of being rescued, of relief – he is out of the water when he had been in it up to his neck, and now I have control of him, I've helped him, I've got him breathing smoothly and securely. It always worked.

Once we'd covered most of the techniques we needed to learn in the docks, we moved on for three days' training at Horsea Island.

I can't say I was thrilled to be back at Horsea. I knew I was going to get cold in my discount suit. I expected to get the same level of crap from the divers there as we'd had when I was on my Ship's Diver's course. I was surprised, though, by our reception; all the senior Clearance Divers gave us a lot of respect for being on that course, and I realized that they respected us for doing the job we did, and this blew me away as I hadn't expected that. After our being dirt on their shoes they were as nice as pie, and we were all of a sudden on first-name terms. I can see it from their point of view, as now I could say that jumping out of an aircraft with a full dive set on is no mean feat; nobody else in the Navy does it.

Horsea Lake is an excellent training place for divers as it's dark, cold and full of stuff you're likely to see at sea — underwater debris, jellyfish, that sort of thing — but it's only a step away from dry land. Those organizing the course have a degree of familiarity with the layout underwater — the position of the Land Rovers, the ambulance, the helicopter, the armoured personnel carrier — so they are able to come up with ways of making the tests we novices have to undergo as tough as possible. You could say I had an unfair advantage, having recently done my Ship's Diver's course there as well, but because the things they wanted to teach us now — the elements of the training that they would want us to be sure about before we could qualify as SAR Divers — were totally different to the training I'd done before, they might as well have been in a completely different place anyway. But everyone who dives in the services ends up in Horsea Lake at one time or another, so we'd all been through it at some point before now.

'What this next exercise is about,' said Steve before

we started that morning in Horsea, 'is learning how to recover casualties who are trapped underwater.' We'd already covered panicking swimmers at the surface – each of us getting a thump in the face for our trouble – so this didn't sound like much fun. 'Andy will be the person you have to recover,' Steve continued, as we groaned. Andy seemed to enjoy making the training that bit harder by creating unforeseen problems as we tried to rescue him. 'He'll be playing the part of some-one whose vehicle has gone into the water, and now needs recovery. You'll have to swim down, locate the vehicle, check Andy's vital signs and then – depending on what you find – exit the vehicle carefully and bring him safely to the surface.' Andy's broad grin grew wider. 'You'll be assessed by Andy on your competencies underwater as well as on the time taken from dive to surface. Any questions?'

There was silence.

'Good. Jay – you're up first.'

I had, by now, ditched my discount suit so at least I wouldn't freeze before I'd even got started. Andy went ahead and disappeared into the murky water just in front of the training platforms. I was to give him a couple of minutes to get into position and then go looking for him.

As usual the visibility was really poor, although I'm sure that Andy had done his best to stir up the silt with his fins as he'd readied himself so that it was harder to see than ever. The cold bit into me almost immediately;

I knew I could ignore it now that I was in a better suit but it still shot into me so that I was forced to move onwards, quickly, to keep some warmth in me.

The Land Rover ambulance was ahead about four metres and down about six metres; I knew this from previous dives. I swam towards it, finning gently and keeping my arms raised just in front of my face so that I wouldn't swim into anything solid without warning. The water was like a thick green soup, and although I could just about make out my hands if they were no more than a few inches in front of me, I had no idea how far I had to go unless I tried to keep some sort of internal measurement going – the number of strokes from my legs, that kind of thing.

The Land Rover appeared out of the muck and gloom as if it had suddenly materialized there and, even though I knew to expect it, I couldn't help but rear back a little in surprise. Little shoals of silver fish fluttered in and out of my vision as I came in closer. I'd come at it from an angle, and had ended up approaching it from the side. I moved along to my right and, sure enough, there was Andy, looking at me as I came towards the front of the vehicle. He was seated in the driver's position, with the door shut. I knew this wasn't going to be as easy as that, though, and – sure enough – when I moved to open the door I discovered that it had been welded shut. When I moved round to the other side of the vehicle, pulling myself across over the bonnet, I saw that although I might have been able to squeeze in,

I would have had trouble ensuring that neither my, nor Andy's, kit was damaged as we came back out again.

I remembered Andy was watching me so made sure I used my air sparingly, breathing in a controlled way as I manoeuvred myself to the back of the ambulance. The doors were missing here so this would be the easiest route in; before I went in, though, I would have to be sure I could find my way out again (not that difficult in this instance but obviously a challenge if I'd entered a sunken ship), so I spooled off some line from the reel I carried with me, my escape line if I went into a sunken aircraft or ship. This was also employed to release a delayed SMB (Surface Marker Buoy). I could mark my route out by trailing a line marked with Cyalumes, the only way in water as murky as this.

Entering the back of the vehicle wasn't a problem although someone had mentioned seeing a moray eel down in the lake recently; I hoped it had found somewhere else to settle. The water in here was stirred around less frequently than in the rest of the lake, so it was thicker and darker – if the rest of the lake was like soup, this was like moss. It was also a lot colder so, once I was out of Andy's sight, I took a couple of deep gulps of air to try and flood my body with warmth – I knew I still had more than enough air to deal with the problems here and then get back to the surface. Gripping the roof, I turned myself upside down and started to pull myself into the space at the back – I wanted to be sure I didn't strike my cylinders and this way I could be sure none of my equipment would hit the top as I went further in.

I slid my way down until I reached the front two seats at which point I turned myself around and grabbed hold of the seat in front of me. It was slimy to the touch but at least there was nothing living on it, like one of the tiny jellyfish that populated the lake. Andy was in the seat to my right and he'd now turned to face me. Peering in closely I could see he was mobile and aware so there was no need to carry out any medical checks; I picked up his right arm and marked out 'OK?' on it – he signalled back he was fine. I pointed first to his neck – no problems moving it – and then his legs – no, they weren't stuck at all. So I moved behind him and lifted him out of the seat, pulling him to the left as I did so.

Andy tried his hardest to be a total dead weight and to be of no help at all, but at least he chose not to fight me. People can panic when a rescuer comes towards them, and part of our training had involved collecting a few bruises from the assistant instructors eager to demonstrate just what that state of panic might force some people to do. I was still floating about in the back, trying to manoeuvre him and at the same time keep my dive set from banging into anything, and I realized I would need to get a stronger purchase if I was to get him out of there. I let my legs drift down until they were touching the bottom of the ambulance – I knew this because of the feeling underneath as well as the clouds of thick silt that bloomed upwards, totally obscuring the little vision I had. Something slithered underneath my foot – I don't know what, but at least it didn't bite.

My right hand still had hold of Andy's left arm. I lifted him up – he was neutrally buoyant so this required no superhuman effort on my part – and gently yanked him towards me. Any diver's course teaches you how to carry a diver so that you can control your movement and use your air properly. In this instance, I couldn't see Andy, but I could tell he was still breathing from the movement so I didn't need to go to any great lengths to share air. I turned him on to his back and backed out carefully, making sure as I reached the back of the ambulance that I swung my legs upwards so as to lie backwards and ensure I didn't crack against anything as we left the vehicle. With one hand I held on to Andy and with the other I grabbed my marker line, and I finned strongly a couple of times to get out of there and shake the cold off me.

As predicted Andy did his best to cause trouble here, his arms and legs catching as we went, so that I had to keep stopping and readjusting my position while I ensured, by touch alone, as I couldn't see much in the thick soup we were swimming in, that he was free of whatever obstruction he'd managed to engineer. This had the irritating additional effect of using up air.

Once we'd cleared the Land Rover visibility improved, not so much that it became clear but certainly a lot better than in the thick green gloom I'd just left. The water around us was now a yellowish colour and if I tipped my head backwards I could see the bright daylight above us. I looked at Andy again; I indicated to him that we would be going to the surface now and he nodded back at me. I glanced first at my air situation and then at his; we had enough air and I made it clear to him that this was going to be okay. I tried to think of anything that I might have missed; I couldn't see that there was anything, so far, that Steve might take issue with. I took Andy's hands and made him grip hold of my stab jacket; grabbing hold of his, I gradually inflated my vest and we rose a little in the water. I took it slowly, knowing that this was part of the purpose of the exercise; if I'd been rescuing someone in a poor physical state who'd been underwater for a period of time, then I would have to be very wary about decompression disorders, such as the bends, affecting them. As I knew Andy hadn't been down for long, and at a relatively shallow depth, I wasn't really worried about this but knew that for the sake of the training I had to act accordingly.

Andy continued to hang unhelpfully and as we rose up he seemed to get heavier – I know this isn't possible, but that's how it felt. At least he wasn't kicking me or trying to punch me. Yet.

Finally we breached the surface and I was able to reach out and grab hold of the side of the boat in which Steve sat. Andy sprang to life and did the same; he looked up at Steve and nodded. I expected a full debriefing there and then, but Steve's only words to me were, 'OK, Jay, next time we'll use Fred and we'll see how you do then.' Thanks a lot.

Going back down again later that morning with Dead Fred was not as straightforward. The dummy was worse because he's negatively buoyant at nine metres and is a real handful to get to the surface. Once I'd got him up it was my job to keep him up. Because I'm a smallish bloke I only had a medium jacket on and with all my weights it just about kept me floating and I was trying to keep Dead Fred afloat by treading water madly as they were debriefing me. I didn't let go but John did, and Dead Fred plummeted down like the dead weight he is into the silt – it took two of them to find him. Thank God I never let go of him.

Once we'd all passed our tests at Horsea the next trip we took was to Yeovilton, to visit the Dunker. This is set up for aircrews – indeed, anyone who flies in or regularly with the military – to learn how to get out from an aircraft if it has crashed into the sea.

The Dunker – properly known as the Underwater Escape Training Unit – is a deep indoor pool into which can be dropped two sorts of helicopter fuselage; it's made available to other organizations as well as the British Armed Forces, so it's used by anyone flying over water – civilians flying out to oil rigs, for instance – so that they can gain the experience of a dunking as part of their training. The interiors of the two bits of fuselage are rigged up to resemble the helicopters most commonly flown – the Lynx in the small one, the Merlin and the Sea King in two halves of the larger unit. The trainees strap themselves into the seats inside the units which are then lowered into the water, usually upside down. The aim is to teach people to get out of their seats and go through the nearest appropriate exit – whether it's a window or a door – before swimming to the surface. Mostly it's done in the dark, to make it more realistic. Crews are trained to use their emergency air supplies, and if there's a problem there are divers stationed at the bottom of the pool to help out. When we were being trained as SAR Divers, the tasks were made harder – obstacles were placed in our way, windows locked shut so we had to turn around and find another exit, that sort of thing. We had to learn how to deal with ejection seats, with canopy releases, and how to help someone escape when they're panicking, fighting back at you.

For some exercises Nic, John and I would be pinned under our seats, or we would be told to leave the aircraft via one exit only, the hardest one to reach of course, and sometimes we would get out only to be told to go back in to find and remove someone else as well – we were put through all sorts of different scenarios, as many as we could physically train for, always trying to push the barriers as much as possible but within the safety of a training environment. It could be claustrophobic, when we were strapped in and the aircraft was lowered into the water in total darkness, and of course everyone has accidents, swimming into windows and doors as well as each other, but I managed it on all the occasions I went through the Dunker. It was a lot less enjoyable when we had to perform the same exercises only this time with no mask on; I could still see a little but it was a lot more blurry and I had to remember not to let water in my nose.

I only had to cope with one serious accident while on the course. It was just my luck; on what was almost my last day of jumping from the aircraft, the helicopter tipped a bit in the breeze as I was waiting for the order to jump and I was jolted out unexpectedly. I tumbled out face first, went smack into the water and smashed my two top front teeth out. I didn't realize what I'd done till I was about four metres down (our plunge depth if we are fully weighted), although I knew something had gone wrong because it really hurt. The piece of skin between my lips and my gums had gone straightaway (it's almost non-existent now although it has grown back a bit) and I had a mouth full of grit and teeth and blood. I climbed into the boat bleeding everywhere – my teeth hadn't just snapped off but were all knurled round and smashed up. 'That looks quite messy' was the helpful remark from one of the instructors, handing me a bucket to wash the blood off the boat. I had to make an emergency appointment with the dentist at Culdrose to put my teeth back together, but, surprise surprise, because I was diving the next day I went through the whole thing in the dentist's chair with no pain relief, as I would have had to have twenty-four hours off after an anaesthetic.

Oddly that wasn't the most painful part of the course. Yes, it hurt and I was in agony for the afternoon and evening, but the constant pain of the freezing cold, and the repetitive nature of the diving, knowing every night I'd have to get up the following morning after the hardest day of my life and do it all over again – only it's going to be even harder because they'll build another aspect into it, and then test me on it – that was the worst part of it all. The last thing I wanted to do was to drop off this course, because it was an easy course to fail – I've seen people who thought they would make brilliant SAR Divers simply take themselves off the course, sometimes right at the start, because it was too much for them. Luckily for me my wife is a trained sports therapist, so she had her elbows in my back and joints every evening, trying to put me back together, because every bit of me was hurting. I was still taking my concoctions of pills at breakfast just to get me through the day. It was all right when I was active, but standing, waiting for Nick or John to have their go, I'd get freezing cold. It was cold in the boat. I'd get warm for a while doing lots of jumps. Then I'd have time to grab a sandwich before getting back in the boat to get cold again: *dive dive dive*. Then it was aircraft jumps, more waiting about in the cold – it was all knackering, with no let-up whatsoever. To complete my nightmare I blew my sinuses every time I dived, so there was always blood about. When I had really sticky sinuses Steve would force-feed me spoonfuls of mustard – it was like being a child again. How horrible to have that taste of English mustard in the back of my throat, but it did do what was needed and cleared my sinuses. I've never much liked mustard anyway but after that I can honestly say I really, really hate mustard.

Finally we reached the last day and the full SAR exercise they'd designed to test us. Naturally because I'd hated working with him so much they put me in with Dead Fred.

The exercise started as every job would do. I was ready in the squadron, waiting for the alarm to go off. They don't actually ring the alarm – that would get everyone's attention and the duty crew need to be ready for genuine emergencies – but someone stuck their head round the door of the Aircrewmen's room, pointed to me and said, 'Alarm. Alarm.' The lads cheered me as I stood up and went to the SAR Ops room to be told what the emergency was: there were reports of a person in Falmouth Bay, it wasn't clear how he'd got there or what condition he was in, we had to fly out and rescue him and take action from there. The point of this exercise wasn't just to test me on what I could do in the water but also to see how I would respond to an emergency I hadn't anticipated and how I'd handle all the aspects of the recovery, from the alarm sounding to standing down at the end of the job.

Once we were fully tasked, and changed, we ran out across the apron and into the helicopter, me lugging my dive kit with me, as I expected to have to use it once we arrived on scene. We flew the ten miles out to Falmouth Bay and went in low to look for our missing person. I was already in my suit, getting ready to jump out into the water, when we spotted him – Dead Fred, that is – by the rocks, all tangled up in a parachute, he was in the worst position I could expect.

This was the first part of the test. All along we'd been practising one thing – jumping out of the aircraft – and suddenly here I was and I couldn't jump, I couldn't dive out on to rocks. I called over the con for the pilot to back away from the scene, and thought quickly about what I should do. This exercise was challenging everything I'd just learned – should I go in on the surface, or sub-surface with full dive set or just a snorkel? My assessors watched as I called out: 'We'll keep the hover here so as to prevent the downwash from the helicopter moving the parachute around at all. I'm going to go down from out here and swim in to rescue the victim. I'll swim back out from the cliff with him and bring him back up to cab from there. Clear?' The pilot signalled back he'd understood; Steve Bielby sat impassively, so I had no idea whether or not he approved of my plan.

I didn't put my dive set on but just slipped my dive mask with a snorkel over my head, connected myself to the winch, and instructed the crewman to lower me down to the water, where I disconnected and swam off in the direction of Dead Fred.

Parachutes are horrible things to encounter in the water: the sodden weight of the material is one thing but it's all the rigging that can cause real difficulties – get yourself tangled up in those and you could die, it's that much of a problem. Luckily we had practised exactly this when training in the Dunker so I was well aware of what I needed to do. Steve had been quite clear in his instructions: 'The way to handle it is first of all not to panic, keep your eyes open, find a seam, follow it. If you follow a seam, you'll get to an end eventually, whereas if you just cut through anywhere you might be in the middle of all of the chute and all of the entanglements.'

My plan was to surface-swim towards the chute and then to dive down so as to swim underneath it and come up at the point where the rocks ran into the sea, minimizing the amount of trouble I might find myself in. As I swam down I reached to pull my dive knife out of its sheath. I was going to rise up slowly with my arms raised above my head to try and find one of the seams, and then follow it out to the edge with my knife when I did so then I could move into the middle through the gap I'd created, allowing me to reach the person in the centre safely.

This plan worked smoothly and I found myself face-to-plastic-head with Dead Fred in a moment; I elected to cut him free from the parachute rather than to untie him as I decided that speed was the correct approach for me to take now. Once he was free of the harness, I slid him gently out to deeper water – one hand behind his head so as to prevent that moving or going underwater – and then manoeuvred myself underneath him so as to support him on the swim back out to the waiting aircraft. Dead Fred was as uncooperative as ever: he had no buoyancy and I had to fin extra hard to keep myself as well as him on the surface. I tired myself out swimming backwards with him out to sea, where the strop was lowered down to me. I took him up in a double-lift harness, and, once back in the aircraft, determined what medical assistance I could give him there and then and where we were going to take him – which hospital was closest – before we returned to the squadron. I was debriefed back in the Ops room before Steve stepped forward, stuck his hand out and said, 'Congratulations. You've passed.'

We had our photos taken, one of them with us behind the standard issue Siebe Gorman diving helmet, circa 1890s, in which many divers' children have been christened (the helmet is taken out to the church and the vicar will fill it with holy water – born to the job, aren't they, then?). Almost all of the SAR Diver's courses 771 ran were held with no more than two or three people; 100 per cent success rates were rare. Nic, John and I were now all fully qualified Royal Navy Search and Rescue Divers.

# 4. Angels in the Guise of Men

I've been rescued myself, once – well, in a way. It was 1988, and I was fifteen and taking part in a charity row in aid of the children's cancer charity CLIC. We were rowing out to Eddystone lighthouse, which stands about thirteen miles south-west of Plymouth. I was in a single-man canoe and there were quite a few of us who set off that morning to head out to the rock, go round the lighthouse, and come back in again. The weather when we initially set out wasn't too bad, but the sea state got worse the further we drew away from land, and by the time we'd got to the lighthouse the swells were pretty big. It took all my energy to keep pushing the paddle through the racing surf. By the time I'd gone another few miles on the return journey – I was probably about six miles offshore – I'd already cap-sized three times. Each time I'd dragged myself back into the boat, but this last time as I bobbed up out of the waves and held on to the canoe I realized that I wasn't going to make it, I had no strength left at all. It wasn't that I couldn't pull myself into the canoe – I couldn't even find the will to right it in the first place. I clung to the side until I was pulled in by the rescue boat, a flat-bottomed landing-craft that had gone out alongside all the canoeists to act as a backup should the weather get bad and it not be possible for all of us to get back – which is precisely what happened. The waves carried on building and building, and more and more people were dragged on board and their canoes tied off at the back. The craft was covered and as it was cold the crew had put the heaters on full blast, but the heaters seemed to be directly connected to the diesel engines, the smell of which filled the interior. The pleasant effect of the warmth was quickly offset by the stench of seasickness, as the craft plunged up and down. In the end I don't think many people actually managed to complete the course and every one of the rescued canoeists ended up vomiting.

So I knew something of what it was like to be whisked away from danger, or from the churning seas into the relative safety of a lifeboat, even if I hadn't experienced being pulled up into the air on the end of a wire into a thundering helicopter.

The first time I really understood what Search and Rescue was all about – what 771 stood for – was a few years after that, when I saw a programme on TV, a part of the BBC's *999* series, about the rescue of crew and passengers from a ship called the MV *Murree*. In true *999* style, they mixed actual footage of the rescue taken from the helicopters with actors dramatizing the events, so the impact it made was immense. Years later I became friends with one of the SAR Divers on that extraordinary job and he was able to fill in a lot more about it than I'd understood from the TV.

It's amazing how close to their own deaths some people go in their voyage to saving other people's lives, and saying that does sound odd coming from someone who does the job I do, but I never think about that when I'm out in the SAR helicopter and risking my life. I obviously think about my own safety and the safety of the others in the crew, but not in the same way as when I'm watching someone else go through the extremes we all face. I suppose it's because at the time we're doing our job, we're doing exactly what we've trained for so we don't have time to stand back and think about it.

Dave Wallace and Steve 'Shiner' Wright, who were both awarded the George Medal for this rescue, were based at Culdrose and worked as SAR Divers and were called out to attend a ship sinking in the Channel. The *Murree* was on her way to Egypt in October 1989, carrying about forty people on board, along with containers strapped tightly down to the deck. The 100 mph winds of the storm meant it stood little chance and, sure enough, the cargo shifted, forcing a hole in the ship's bow. A distress call was sent out, alerting the Coastguard that it was about twenty-five miles off Start Point in Devon. Three helicopters flew out, including two from Culdrose. Dave and Shiner were winched down and started getting the passengers up and into the waiting Sea Kings. Among the passengers were some women with very small children. The only way for the two divers to get them safely into the helicopter was for the women to be winched up in a twin-strop alongside either Dave or Shiner, with the baby in the grip of the diver. Dave told me years later that one of the babies wriggled the whole way up, all eighty feet, and that was about the worst thing he could imagine happening on a rescue – losing a baby at that height. It was only when he'd safely handed the baby over to its mother inside the cab that he realized he hadn't taken a breath the whole way up on the cable.

Dave went back down on the deck to continue removing passengers, amidst the fury of the storm as it lashed the ship, sending walls of icy water slapping into them as they struggled to maintain their balance. The two divers carried on clearing the passengers and crew, until there were only about four left. If this sounds orderly, it wasn't; the water was rising fast around them, and just when it seemed the end was in sight there was a thunderous crashing below, probably the moment when the hull finally gave way under the pressure, and the ship lurched. Hastily they slipped the strops over the last people on deck and helped get them into the helicopters, holding on to the highlines – used to stablize the winch cable itself – as the rising crewmen danced about in the gusting winds.

Then they noticed that the winch operators were agitatedly signalling to them to get off the ship, and, just as they realized their time was up, the *Murree* swivelled

90 degrees, sending the two men sliding down the deck, so they both scrambled across to the guard rails at the side, readying themselves to jump into the sea.

This was where the nightmare kicked in. Dave's foot curled round a rope and he had to stop and bend down to release himself, even as the sea started opening up below him, a dark toothless mouth, swirling everything in its path down its gullet, ready to swallow the *Murree* and everything on it – including him. He tugged his foot free and went to the side to follow Shiner overboard. Without a glance, he threw himself over.

It was just as well he hadn't looked down, as the fall from the ship, now tilting at an improbably angle, had risen so high in the waves that he dropped nearly one hundred feet before hitting the sea. The force knocked the air out of him as he sank down into the dark, freezing water; as soon as he could summon the strength, though, he fought his way back up to the surface, but that didn't make him safe – high above him rose the stern of the sinking ship and spinning directly above his head was the propeller screw, roaring above the crash of the waves, deafening both divers – and threatening to come crashing back down on them. Dave Wallace told me that at this moment he was the most frightened he had ever been in his whole life.

They both had to move away from there as fast as they could. Swimming away might not be enough, though, for, as the *Murree* was going down, the whirlpool created by her descent could have taken them down into the depths too. Dave and Shiner had to swim fast for all they were worth away from the ship, desperate now to save themselves. As soon as they were at a safe enough distance, the helicopters lowered lines to winch them both back into the aircraft.

The story had a more than happy ending, though. Once they were back on board, one of the rescued Pakistani crewmen, the Second Officer, leant over to them both. 'Thank you, thank you,' he said, as he pressed his lifejacket into their hands. They nodded their appreciation and looked down at it. He'd found a pen and had written a message on the lifejacket. The men read it and didn't know what to say – they were so moved. The words written in a helicopter, by a soaked and exhausted man, as a tribute to his rescuers, read:

> To the angels who came in the guise of men. The Lord hath chosen thee to perform the most profound of his miracles – save life.
>
> You are what the world was made for.

For years that lifejacket hung in the stairwell at 771, reminding everyone of this extraordinary rescue. It's gone now.

Trophies and memorials from many of the jobs that 771 has been involved with over the years line the stair-cases and hallways in our building. When I first joined the squadron, they were a record of extraordinary and daring rescues carried out by my colleagues, old and new, and as I walked past I would always look at them and imagine what the men and women involved had been through to have earned those stirring records.

When I first thought about joining 771, I wasn't aware of the variety of jobs I'd be expected to carry out. If I had in my mind a heroic figure leaping on to the deck of a storm-tossed ship every day then I was very surprised that the first few times I flew out it was to places inland. In a rural environment like Cornwall snow and floods can leave people as isolated as any ship stranded in the ocean, and the only way help can get to them, sometimes, is from the air. The summer I joined, huge storms sent millions of gallons of rainwater surging in a devastating ten-foot wall through the town of Boscastle, the river burst its banks and buildings collapsed, seventy cars were washed out to sea, and people had to be evacuated off their own rooftops. We were called out to assist, along with all the other available helicopter units in Cornwall, and even had to break through tiled roofs to get to people to lift them out of the way of the flood. Over one hundred people were eventually airlifted to safety. Jobs like these have additional complications for everyone in the aircraft, with the dangers of flying into power cables a real threat at such low levels over the valleys and higher ground of the moors. It's not just the pilots who have to keep an eye out for them; it's also us in the back, leaning out of the open door to help with spotting the pylons – particularly in poor visibility or even at times when we have to wear night-vision goggles to see them.

The following winter saw further extremes in the weather, and we had record snowfalls throughout the county. Normally snow isn't a problem for helicopter-rescue services – the aircraft can continue flying, provided the landing apron is kept clear – but it's the related difficulty – ice – that everyone in the squadron has to watch out for. This particular winter we were caught out by a double-whammy, not just the amount of snow that fell but also the extensive length of the big freeze. Some of the squadron had only just returned from a week away on some military tasking, and we'd watched the weather coming in from the north while we were out at sea up there. When we landed back at Culdrose the snow was so thick in the surrounding area we shut down. I managed to lock my keys in the car, with the engine running and the alarm going, so I couldn't leave the base. I rang my wife Louise and asked her to drive out with the spare keys; I wish I hadn't. She nearly lost control driving down the hill where we lived and when she had the car safely in gear she saw a petrol tanker slide all the way down the hill towards her and the baby. She said when she reached the base: 'I don't know how it missed us but it just drifted past me at about 10 mph, the driver sat inside his cab, waving people away . . .' I sat her down, told her she wasn't budging, and that I wasn't coming home just yet. Things were so bad out there that we had five aircraft airborne and instead of being sent home I was being re-tasked.

The snow was so thick that people had abandoned their cars on the moors, but the ambulances couldn't get out to them as there was a tremendous amount of snow and fog, so it was left up to us. One of the squadon's aircraft came down in a field by the town of Liskeard with a fuel problem, and we tried to deliver an engineering team to them but couldn't get near. They landed with a 'fuel-indication problem' – but the crew didn't know if it was a faulty indicator or if the aircraft had dumped all its fuel so they had to land there and then. Those are the rules, so that's what they had to do and, as luck would have it, the field was right opposite a pub. They were welcomed in but of course they couldn't drink because they were the duty crew. To make matters worse, they'd launched with most of the SAR equipment – the usual procedure in normal times, but not in this instance. I'd argued with Spike Hughes, the Aircrewman on board, saying that as there weren't enough SAR kits to go round – there were five aircraft flying but we only had enough kit for three – we needed to share some of the equipment with the other aircraft. The duty Aircrewman's point was that, as the duty crew, they were going to need the kit. Spike won the argument and then sat in a field while the rest of us flew about performing all the rescue missions.

We had a very busy few days and the engineers

worked hard to make sure that we had as many aircraft as possible flying, in conditions as dire as any I'd seen in Cornwall. One trip, for instance, started when we flew to a field to pick up 500 blankets and sleeping bags from a dozen coppers who pulled them out of a lorry to chuck them into the back of the aircraft – I'd never seen the aircraft so full, I couldn't see any part of it, I couldn't even see the pilots. We had to fly at a low enough level to see where we going to with the load, navigating our way through the snow flurries using night-vision goggles, to a football pitch where we had to unload everything. Then we had to fly back to Culdrose to collect and drop off more supplies at the hostels on the moors because they couldn't get anything moving on the roads at all. On the way back, we had to divert to carry out some emergency calls because the ambulances couldn't get through – things like a heart-attack victim in Padstow.

It was a manic few days and it left most of us exhausted, coming back from exercise and going straight out on rolling shifts – but it was exhilarating, it was all what we call 'reactive tasking': going from one call to another, sometimes not returning to base in between each action. That showed me early on some of the best of the squadron; the rest of the base was quiet but 771 was able to launch because we had engineers manning the machines, de-icers and tractors out on the apron constantly trying to keep our dispersal clear. The paramedics who worked for the local ambulance service came to fly with us instead of travelling out and about by ambulance. They'd all jumped into one big 4x4 and got in just before all the roads were blocked. It was a good team effort; they were distributed between all the aircraft as we were tasked from job to job through the Falmouth Coastguard: 'Right, get a crew, go: no time to brief, okay, it's that way.' That taught me a lot of what SAR's all about – it needn't involve the sea but it still means carrying out life-saving rescues.

Other jobs I've done since have involved life-saving without even stepping out of the aircraft: we've transported patients on the organ-transplant list from Treliske to London, a paramedic along with the patient in order to keep a check on their stability during the flight. We fly into London and to the hospital where the surgery will take place, using the River Thames as our marker for the route in.

A more familiar part of our work here, something visitors see when they come down to the south-west in the summer, is when we have to rescue people from cliffs. Mostly the people we fly out to are at the bottom of the cliff because they've fallen, but not always. We do get a number of people who climb up the cliff, 'showing off to the wife', but get to a certain point and then can't cope with the height and go rigid – they'll stay put somewhere until we come along and help to get them down. Cliff-stickers, they're known as, someone who's overly confident and then realizes they're not overly competent and gets stuck. We have to try and pick them off without knocking them down, so the aircraft has to be at a high level to reduce the downdraft and the Air-crewman has to be manoeuvred into them from the side or from down below – we don't come in from above as they might get nudged off as we come down and then they'd fall. We can't put a strop on them over their head because they'd lose their grip, but instead we use an 'open becket' method so that we're able to put the strop around their middle, and then lift them off and take them either down to the beach or up to the cliff top, whichever is the safer.

One of the reasons we have to be careful when try-ing to winch someone off a cliff is the reflection off the cliff of the downwash – the force that the rotor blades send below to provide the 'cushion' of air that helps the aircraft fly. The downwash comes down from the blades in a cone-like effect, so if the pilot takes the heli-copter too close in to the cliff then the air pushed downwards will hit the cliff and bounce back out – the reflection buffeting the rescuer in a way that turns him into a human pendulum. That swing can become dan-gerous. When we get novice or trainee pilots who are a bit what's known as 'agricultural' on the controls – like a learner driver grinding the gears – that's when they can induce a swing. Two foot of movement in the heli-copter can be like twenty foot down on the end of the winch, so if it started happening when we were by a cliff, I would brace myself and ready my feet to push off from the wall if I started to swing into it. And when we touch down at base again, I'll have a few words with the pilot – very much off the record.

People like to watch the cliff rescues and sometimes we have our suspicions about them. We had a call once to go out, the helicopter put the Aircrewman down on the beach and he walked over to the group gathered by the cliff. There was a young woman standing just above head height on a small shelf jutting out from what looked to be more like a low rock than a cliff. The Aircrewman looked in irritation at the people waiting expectantly for him to winch her down; instead he just reached up, grabbed her foot, said, 'Look, you lot, you can do this, just grab her bloody legs and pull her down, it's not a job for us, that.'

I am wary of cliff rescues, and that's because of my problems with heights. As I'm cautious of going any-where near something high, when we go to rescue cliff-stickers – and I've done a few of those – I couldn't understand what had changed for them, why they could go out on a cliff and then get stuck, when I wouldn't go out at all if I felt like that. Until, that is, I was talked into going climbing myself once with two very experienced climbers. I ended up holding on with the tips of my fingers and toes, with no ropes and a sheer drop of hundreds of feet below me. I was pretty unhappy to be up there, but I did it, and although I nearly froze, and now fully understand why people freak out and cannot physically move, I still did it. I guess I didn't like the feeling that a sense of absolute fear could rule what

I wanted to do. I know that a natural fear – a natural awareness – is there for a reason, but I refuse to let it govern me.

Worse, though, than cliffs and the potential for falls are those rescues where the sea enters caves. Here the problems can be greater than in the open because, obviously, the helicopter cannot be above waiting to rescue the victim or the Aircrewman. It's in these rescues that the true value of the SAR Diver's intense training starts to show itself. My friend Bungi Williams went on a job that won him and the rest of the crew awards, at Mawgan Porth, on the north coast of Cornwall. A lifeguard had gone wandering with a friend of his who'd only the day before flown in from New Zealand during a stormy period one summer and she'd been swept off her feet by a rip tide and taken rapidly away from the beach. On the eastern side of Mawgan Porth, around the corner from the beach, there is a double set of caves on the edge of the point that the two of them had had to swim into in order to take shelter from the tide and the wind.

The search, with about a hundred people looking for them, went on for eleven hours before they were eventually located, so the tide had gone through to high and was by then dropping back again. At just past midnight, when the search party had made a decision that they would stand down until the tide had dropped right back, and resume searching later, and the crew were ready to fly back to Culdrose in the expectation they'd be needed for another shout, they were radioed by the RNLI – the missing pair had been heard screaming in the water. The lifeguard was then spotted swimming out of one of the caves, was dragged on to the RNLI's boat and quickly provided information as to the whereabouts of the girl and also of her condition – she was suffering from hypothermia. The RNLI radioed up to the helicopter, and a plan was made: the pilot would fly in as close as possible to the cliff-face, with the rotors no more than five feet from the rocks – a tricky enough task in broad daylight but a real challenge in the dark – and then swing Bungi in at the same time as he was lowered down. The plan was dependent upon Bungi's skills as a SAR Diver – any other Navy rescuer would have had to remain attached by a line to the ship they'd come from, which would necessarily limit their range and abilities once in the caves.

The plan worked, and Bungi disconnected from the winch and waded in, chest-deep; the sea inside the cave was far rougher than in the open and he was thoroughly bashed about, knocked from one side to the other on the rocks. Unfortunately, as soon as he'd entered the water, his radio had gone down – they were supposed to be waterproof but the extremes of weather the squadron faced down in the south-west appeared to get the better of them – so nobody knew where he was or what was happening once he'd swum into the cave. He had to search for the missing woman for about twenty minutes, in the pitch black, with only his hand-held torch, over jagged rocks and amid churning waves, until he found her over a hundred feet in, right at the back of the cave. The water had risen quite high earlier in the day so she'd been immersed during the high tide. By now it was about one in the morning and as she was only in a shortie wetsuit Bungi quickly checked her over for signs of exposure. She was dazed and hypothermic. She'd been battered against the rocks, so her legs and hands were bruised and cut and she seemed too far gone to make her way out under her own steam so Bungi ended up having to pick her up and carry her out of the cave, back the way he'd come, over the exposed rocks and boulders.

All the way out of the cave Bungi was concerned about the roof – it was being heavily battered, twice daily, by the sea, and he wasn't sure whether or not chunks of rock were going to fall on them as they made their way out. Eventually he did reach the front of the cave, where two RNLI lifeguards swam in to help him; Bungi signalled to the aircraft with his flashlight, they lowered the strop down and she was taken out of the water and was quickly on her way to hospital.

Bungi was awarded the Billy Deacon Award for Bravery, an award named after a coastguard who had been swept overboard in 1997 carrying out a rescue in the Shetland Isles and drowned.

Another thing I learned once I was settled in to my

new role as an SAR Diver was how the Aircrewmen always talked through things that went badly, just to see if there was anything that could be learned from what had occurred to prevent it from happening again in the future. It's useful to understand how someone did something in case that was your first instinct too, and you needed to know that so you could avoid the same outcome. I learned a lot through these de-briefing sessions, and someone who was a fixture of many of them was the previously mentioned Dave Rigg.

Dave Rigg was, thanks to his experience, one of the people who had seen – and dealt with – most things, and his knowledge of how to handle things when they went wrong was very helpful to me and a lot of the lads as they came through. I wouldn't want to suggest Dave is some wise old hand but he's very experienced, and though we rib each other all day long, we need to have someone to discuss what's gone on so as to be sure we can do better next time.

A problem that has come up and which we discuss endlessly is the issue of when – and when not – to cut the cable when there's a person on the end who – if the cable's not cut – might well end up being seriously hurt. There are two systems in the helicopter for cutting the cable: one's near the winch housing and the other is a switch near the pilots. One grim night, Dave was winching a medic down on to the deck of a ship when, just as the doctor touched down, a heavy wave crashed against the side of the boat. The ship lurched down and away, and the sudden movement meant that the doctor was lifted off his feet and yanked across the boat. Dave saw that the doctor was getting dragged into and over the guard rails. If the cable was tangled up in the rails, then it would pull on the aircraft – and the boat – and anything trapped in between, like the doctor, would suffer horribly. So he called out, 'Cut! Cut!' but as he soon as he said it he saw the doctor had managed to get safely away from the guard rails, shipside, and so quickly yelled, 'No! Don't Cut!' and luckily the pilots didn't get to the switch that time, so the doctor was still attached to the wire. Apart from the bruising and dunking the doctor would have suffered, the chances are because it was a night job as well they would have lost him in the darkness with no hope of finding him once he'd drifted away from the boat. He would have had a light on his lifejacket – we all carry one, and also a strobe light in our survival pockets, for just such an emergency – but he'd only have turned one of these lights on when entering the water, and for that he'd have to have been conscious. If someone's gone over the side of a boat, it's often because they've hit something so they could easily be unconscious. Dave now realized that he'd got between fifty and a hundred feet of cable that was dangling down in the water and had gone slack; and because it was dark, with the cable underneath the helicopter, he couldn't tell if the doctor himself had released the cable. It's a horrible feeling, not knowing if someone's there or not, so he started raising the winch slowly, so as not to jar anything, until the wire went taut and the man suddenly swung plumb beneath him. 'The relief surging through me, and the rest of the crew, was something else,' Dave said to all of us when he got back.

It's no joke going into the water that far out to sea, whether you're still attached to the wire or not. The water – if it gets into your suit – is freezing and a two-hour journey back to base in a wet and cold suit is not pleasant. Everyone gets dunked in the ocean once in a while, though, and Dave's experience was one we all talked about because it involved the possibility – something we all fear – of meeting a propeller once in the water. Dave Rigg was out on a long-ranger, not far off the operational range of the Sea King; an accident that far out would be the end of someone – you'd very likely be dead long before you reached land, if the injury was bad enough. The casualty was on a big ship but the weather meant it was just as rough on board as if he'd been in a dinghy, although at least it was daylight. The injury to the crewman was straightforward – he'd fractured his leg – and he was safely strapped into a stretcher and lifted up to the helicopter without incident. It was what happened next that preyed on all our minds. Dave, having played butler down below, carrying the man's bag and a thick coat, was getting ready to return to the sky himself. The boat's crew – eager to help – held on to the highline as Dave connected up to the winch, but they were a little too eager and held it too tightly. Dave slid forward as the winch wire went taut and was jerked backwards as the wire went up, twisting him upside down.

The winch op later told Dave he watched what happened with mounting horror: 'I saw you go, I watched you just miss the guard rail, I thought I'd killed you. As soon as you hit the water the cable just went slack, I thought it had parted and you'd gone.'

Dave had gone sweeping over the guard rails, his head just missing the metal bars by inches, before turning to the side to see a fifty-foot-high wall of water coming towards him – he barely had time to gulp some air in before it hit him. His being bounced around by the water, plunging up and down in the wave, explained how it must have seemed to the winch man that Dave was no longer attached to the cable, but he was. 'I saw just about every colour of water possible, blue, black, green, white, and all that's in my head is: where the hell's the ship's propeller?'

What worried Dave – what worried all of us when we thought about the possibility of such a thing happening to any one of us – was that he had been taken off the boat when it was at the bottom of the trough, rather than at the peak, which meant that the ship would be sitting deeper in the water as it rose around it. 'I knew the ship was coming back up, and I was properly worried – I thought I might get mangled here. I'd come off the back, and I'd just come clear of the boat when I'd hit this thing. I was under, and under, and I thought . . . am I ever going to break the surface?'

The wave did move on, and the winch operator told Dave once he was safely back in the aircraft that as they all stared down to see what was happening to him, all of a sudden Dave came out of the water like a Polaris missile, *kapow*, stunned by the cold – but still holding on to the casualty's jacket and bag.

Dave was recovered to the aircraft but it was only then that he realized that when he went into the waves upside down the icy Atlantic water had found a break in the seal around his neck. His suit had left him wet and freezing. With the patient stabilized, Dave sat there, getting colder and colder on the two-hour journey home. Although it was warm in the back of the aircraft when the door was shut, once the suit had been breached he couldn't get warm, the icy water saw to that. Dave couldn't even risk taking it off and drying out before putting it back on, because if the aircraft ditched – and that was a possibility, given the distance they'd had to travel to the job – then he would be ser-iously exposed and wouldn't last more than a few minutes in the ocean.

When Dave got back and told us all about that one, we all had a laugh – no one was hurt, apart from the casualty and he had been rescued and taken to hospital – and then we all scuttled off to check our dry-bags were fully functioning and there was no chance of the seal breaking. Our normal outfits, worn by the aircrew in the back, are what we call our 'orange bags' – they're light and it's easy to move about wearing them. The old ones we had were useless after they'd been in the water; these new ones are rinsed off when we return to base and they're good to go the next day.

It would have been no joke in the water for the medic at that temperature. We have a cut-off point for the winter; once the air temperature dips below 15°C, we are obliged to wear our rubber-sealed immersion suits when we fly, and that applies to everyone in the aircraft – passengers as well as crew. With the chill factor to take into account, if someone went into the ocean and they didn't have one of those suits on, they'd be lucky to survive an hour. If the temperature sinks lower than that, down to below 10°C, then the time they can survive in the water without a suit drops dramatically – as little as five to ten minutes – because hypothermia will set in that quickly, and once it does the person in the water starts to become disorientated. Once they don't know what they're doing, where to head for safety, they're in real trouble. Even in winter I started sweating as soon as I stepped into mine; in the summer months I don't need to wear it, but in springtime the suit quickly becomes a bugbear. The sea's temperature is always two months behind the ambient air temperature, because it takes such a long time to warm up, so summer will begin, the days start to warm up – we might even have the odd heatwave coming in, when 30°C outside-air temperatures aren't unknown – and we're still in our thick rubber suits, and I learned very quickly that going up and down cliffs to carry out a rescue can give you a really good work-out. I think every time I get a dunking in the winter, though, I'm very glad to have that suit on and will put up with a few sweaty days to have its protection when it's needed.

I realized this the time I was nearly washed off a boat just before Christmas after I'd been at the squadron a couple of years. I'd been put down on the deck of a foreign trawler to take off a crewman who needed hospital treatment. The weather was awful. I'd prepared the casualty by taking him to the bow of the ship and then making him sit down. I was going to take him to the aircraft in a double-lift harness where one strop goes under his legs and the other under his arms, and I indicated to him how I wanted him to stay while he was lifted up: 'Arms must be here' – while I slapped my sides – 'always, okay?' I had everything ready to go and the winch hook was lowered down to me. I had literally a second to get it hooked on. It's important not to hook the patient on before they're ready to be lifted up in case there's a problem, and I was waiting for that second as I had to pick my spot. I could see that there was a massive wave coming to us and as it was only a small trawler, the ship was popping up and down like a cork in a washing machine. Somehow the wave rushing towards us hit the side of the boat and spun it sideways so that instead of the water rushing past the sides of the ship it swept over the top. As I stood there this

barrage of icy water came and swept me off my feet
and across the deck, at some speed, and I was about to
go *whoosh* off the bow and into the sea. Instinctively I
reached out and just stopped myself from going over
the side, grabbing the guard rail as I went past, nearly
yanking my arm out of its socket in the process. Water
that cold – even though it didn't go into my suit, thank
goodness – still gave me an instant headache as I went
under and when I came up out of the wave every part
of my face and scalp felt rubbed raw. I pulled myself
back upright, wondering what had happened to the casualty only to see that he was fine because he was tucked
in against the bow's head, with the winch hovering
above him. I started shaking myself, trying to get the
cold water out of my ears, while the injured crewman
looked at me as if I was the one in trouble: 'All right?'
he said in his broken English.

Many of the ships we landed on were crewed by foreign sailors with little or no grasp of English. The
Captain might be in a position to call over the radio
for assistance, but when I landed on a boat, often the
Captain would have to remain in the wheelhouse and
I'd be left trying to explain the double-strop technique to a bewildered and injured seaman. I learned a
number of handy phrases but most of the time it was
gestures – showing them where I would put the strop
and indicating that they had to remain in that position
all the way up to the aircraft. Sometimes, though, this
wasn't enough. I had a case where the patient, an Afri-

Defence Diving School, Horsea Island.

Me on the Ship's Diver's Course, exhausted, ready for another dip in the cold water.

Aircrew's Survival Course in the New Forest: we're about to go on the run for a week, feeding ourselves from the land. I'm at the back, fourth from the left, and Nobby is in the middle (also at the back), with the blond hair.

We used this diver tank on Air Days and Navy Days; we'd play noughts and crosses with kids on the outside, drawing with chinagraphs on the glass.

The SAR Divers crest – a symbol of hope.

Backing into the aircraft – the winch operator bringing me onboard, but under strict instructions not to touch my kit.

Unweighted jump on a ditched aircrew recovery.

A fish-eye view: the welcome sight of help from above.

Fully equipped, on recovery to the aircraft.

My full SAR kit:

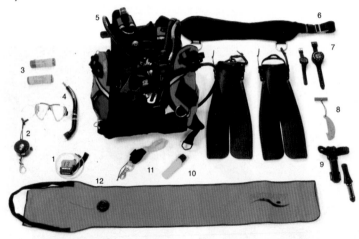

1. Diver rescue beacon. The tube, worn round my neck, glowed blue and the unit radioed a tonal distress signal; 2. Buddy reel, used to mark off my entry – and exit route – from submerged craft; 3. Day/night flares; 4. Mask and snorkel; 5. Breathing Apparatus Search and Rescue. The light on my right shoulder was as bright as an aircraft beacon; 6. Lead-shot weight belt; 7. Compass and dive computer; 8. J-knife, for cutting straps; 9. Diver's knife and sheath; 10. Waterproof torch; 11. Buddy line, 1½ metres long: I'd attach one end to myself and the other round the wrist of the person being rescued; 12. Delayed Surface Marker Buoy.

A forty-foot jump. Our maximum – most of the time.

The *Napoli*, already in trouble. A French Super Frelon helicopter circles around.

The stern started shipping loads of water, prompting the crew to abandon ship.

Taken by the French, this shows the sea state with the waves lining up to bash the lifeboat.

Rescue 194 moving into position.

The *Napoli* lifeboat. These pictures are taken from our video cameras, showing the moment one of the crew was plucked out of the raging sea and into Rescue 194. The lifeboat is barely visible through the white horses.

A proud day at
Buckingham Palace
with Louise and
my QGM.

Another happy
ending to a job
that went well.

can sailor, had been helpfully dosed up by his crewmates – only none of them could tell me what they'd given him.

It was on a gas ship – one carrying tanks of liquefied natural gas – so instead of vast containers stacked on top of one another there were huge tanks surrounded by metal walkways everywhere. I had gone deep into the ship, following someone down ladders and metal stairways as we went further into the bowels, down three decks to where the African deckhand lay. He'd fallen in the high seas and had really hurt his back; in addition, he possibly had some internal injuries – it was hard to tell as he was pretty far gone from all the medicine he'd taken. The crew had given him loads of pills to help with the pain – one of the problems that stems from the ships travelling all over the globe is that they have access to all sorts of different drugs – but no one on board had said, hang on, will these do him any good? Ranged beside his bunk were all sorts of packets and bottles, most of them covered in writing I didn't even recognize. I asked, 'What have you given him?' The guide who'd led me there gestured to the heap of drugs so I had to ask if I could gather them into a bag. 'I have no idea what these are, but they look really bad. I'll have to take them with me to show the doctors, okay?'

I had to get the patient strapped on to a stretcher and then get that delivered to the deck. One of the advantages of being unfamiliar with the interiors of boats meant that it was easier to get the crew to do this part of the task – they'd know where they were going – rather than having to do it myself. So I organized a couple of guys to heave him up and take him along, as gently as they could, while I scooped the drugs into a plastic sack one of them had found for me. Our little group set off, up and down these walkways and ladders, until I saw – above our heads – that there were ventilation grilles cut through. I pointed to one, and by waving my arms about made it plain that I thought the patient would be better off if we could get him to the deck quickly – let's open up these grilles, turn the stretcher into a vertical position, and lift him through. They complied, and within moments he was on top and ready to be lifted up into the helicopter.

Before he went up, however, I had to quickly tell the Observer how we were going to come up to the helicopter. I'd practised in my training for this – in fact we practised it so often it was almost second nature – but I needed to check with him that he was prepared. It's tricky, coming up to an aircraft with a stretcher; do you come up alongside the stretcher, next to the aircraft, and back in, then pulling the stretcher in after you? Do you come up on the other side of the stretcher, so that the patient is the first one to enter into the aircraft? These sound like silly things but it's the kind of detail we have to have in our minds all the time; to get something like that wrong could mean all sorts of problems and if the patient is in a bad state as it is, some mucking about while they're hanging eighty feet above a storm-tossed sea isn't going to help their state of mind, to say the least.

As it is I'm too short to bring it in out-board, so I came up in-board, with my back to the aircraft. The Observer handling the winch then helped me pull the stretcher in as I walked it down into the cab. We flew back and landed at the hospital. The crewman turned out to be okay, once the doctors had managed to work out what cocktail of pills he'd be given from the handfuls of packets and bottles I took in with the patient to show them.

I also learned how to deal with the long-distance journeys out to sea. It's not just about the journey there – it's useful for us to know what sort of boat we're going to, what the sea state is, and as much as we can about the nature of the rescue we're going to undertake. If we're travelling far out to sea on a job, we contact the Aeronautical Rescue Co-ordination Centre (ARCC) at Kinloss and ask them to send Rescue 51 – a Nimrod – ahead of us, because as it's a jet it will get there faster than us. The Nimrod crew can locate the vessel, so that we can go straight to it rather than fly around looking for it – it can be hard to find a vessel at night in the open ocean. The Nimrod will also talk to the vessel's Captain, and, if they speak enough English down there, can gather more advance information on how the patient is faring. For the paramedics on board, that's vital; it gives them a chance to prepare properly for what they have to face the moment they get to the patient.

Along with Dave Rigg, the squadron has another fully trained paramedic, Jason Bibby. 771 no longer carries doctors out on the shouts with the crew, but changes in our approach to the health of those we rescued meant some in the squadron came to be fully trained in the paramedic's role. Thanks to the training they've received, as soon as they're back in the aircraft they can get to work on the patient.

Not that every patient wants to leave their boat and travel to safety in a helicopter, though. One job I was involved in was when Rescue 193 had been called out to Padstow; a yachtsman had been in the water and was suffering from hypothermia. When we arrived on the scene, the RNLI boat was alongside the yacht; when I went below the lifeboat guys were with the patient and I saw almost immediately that he was shivering and seemed to be in the early stages of hypothermia; also he was complaining of a back injury sustained a few weeks before. I thought that between us we would be able to get him easily up on deck and then fly him quickly to hospital; however, he refused to be moved.

Perhaps the back injury he'd sustained put him off being winched up, but he did agree that he needed to get to hospital. I explained that I'd put him in a vacu-mattress, which cocoons the patient, and once he'd seen he wasn't going to be going up into the air on can-vas and poles he relented. We took him up to the aircraft smoothly and transferred him to the hospital; it's not often we come to rescue someone and they refuse our help – when it does happen it's usually a surfer, who always thinks he's better off in the water, no matter how rough it is, and never wants to leave his board behind.

Over the years I've worked a lot with the guys in the RNLI; 771 makes sure that we train regularly with them, and we will stage specific exercises that teach both sides how to work together so as to get the best out of us all. My favourite exercise with them was the RIB transfer; I would jump out of the aircraft when it was at a height of about forty feet, and wait for the ILB – the inshore lifeboat – to pick both me and the exercise casualty up. The ILB would then move under the aircraft, aiming to position itself directly below the winch hook, with both the boat and the helicopter travelling at about 15 knots. This is no mean feat and requires a good coxswain, because it can go horribly wrong in no time at all. When the ILB was correctly positioned underneath the winch hook, I'd attach to it and get winched up on to the aircraft with the casualty. It can be a bit nerve-wracking for the casualty, especially if there are big swells, but it's often the fastest way of ferrying someone to hospital.

Another way of getting a boat to the scene is a Gemini lift, which is when we fly the Navy Gemini inflatable boat out closer to a shout, with the boat hanging below the helicopter. The coxswain and bowman remain in the aircraft and as we approach the scene they get winched into the boat, and start their engine so that 771's pilot (under guidance from the winch operator) can lower the boat, which detaches and speeds off, all in one slick movement. It's great to watch and fun to do, although steering the boat as it is picked up by the helicopter can be a headache. The coxswain needs to keep the boat moving to keep station on the aircraft, because the helicopter needs forward movement to keep steady and safe, so they both move at about 10 knots or so. I've done it, but I had to learn to ignore the effects of the downwash and instead concentrate on getting the power and direction right.

We need to work with the RNLI crews because we will sometimes step in to help them and they will sometimes step in to help us. One time the duty helicopter was called out to a rescue of a yacht just off the coast; it was a filthy day, the rain pouring down, with high winds up to 60 mph battering the water; the seas were pretty big, about twenty-foot swells. What marked this one out was the yacht itself – the main mast must have stood fifty feet high, making a descent down to the deck a very hazardous undertaking. The yacht's pumps had failed so the boat was slowly but surely filling up with the water washing over the side; when the lifeboat came alongside the RNLI managed to get two of its men on board but the seas were too heavy for them to be recovered back to the life raft. We were called out there and I was lowered down to winch them up; that giant mast swinging about in the poor conditions was very worrying indeed but we decided to lower me from sixty feet, so I had the mast in view all the way down –

as it was daylight I could at least see what I was doing clearly and knew that I could avoid any danger easily enough. It would have been a very different story at night in the dark.

I managed to lift them all off and then the RNLI were able to tow the boat into harbour; the RNLI crew vehemently said it was 'the worst shout [they'd] been on in years and certainly the worst ever in June'.

Often what we do is made more dangerous by the design of the boats we have to work with – because the boats aren't usually built to be boarded from directly above. One of the most dangerous hazards we face at sea is on the yachts, for the halyards that rise up from the decks to the tops of the masts can part the winch wire. I've had some very close calls – bashes and bruises but I've been lucky, so no broken bones, yet – but winchmen have died as a result of getting wrapped in the halyards, although not recently I'm glad to say. We're all very much aware of this as a potential problem when we're approaching yachts, and I don't suppose I was ever more aware of this than when I was being lowered on to a racing yacht where the mast must have stood at more than seventy or even eighty feet high, so the aircraft – in order to remain at a safe height above it, given the way the swell could force the boat upwards – was hovering at about a hundred feet. One of the novice sailors had been knocked unconscious by the boom and needed to come off – he'd come round but had quite a bad head injury, as the boom was huge, one foot by a foot, but if someone's unconscious from a head injury we always want to bring them in for a check-up at least. The waves were so big the boat was being thrown all over the place, it was horrific weather again – 50-knot winds – and of course it was at night.

We talked to the yacht's crew to get them steering in the right direction, to take the sails down and get everything secured. On this particular flight we had an Aircrewman, Ian Stables, who was in the middle of his SAR course, and Ian looked out of the door and said, 'You're not doing this, are you?'

I peered outside to see what had made him say that. The helicopter was very high up above the boat, about the same as if I were standing on top of a ten-storey building. The yacht was pitching and rolling about furiously below us, its giant mast waggling underneath the helicopter, like a drunk trying hopelessly to stab us. The wind was pushing into us almost horizontally and all around was dark. If I was going to compile a list of dangerous issues to be confronted by on a job, this one would have ticked just about every box. I turned back towards Ian and grinned at him. 'Oh yes,' I said.

He couldn't believe it. 'You've got to be joking!' Out I went, with 'Chuck' Norris, the Observer, as the winch op. We tried for ages to get a highline on, but the closest we came to getting it attached was when it got wrapped around the mast and parted, which left about 150 feet of terylene rope, about a centimetre in diam-eter, stretched out horizontally from the top of the mast – that's how strong the wind was blowing. Another complication, then, for the pilot to avoid.

Meanwhile the yacht – fully lit up to help me board it – was being shoved hard from one side to the other as the waves came out of the darkness to strike the sides, again and again, and I was becoming more and more apprehensive the longer I hung there, the roaring sea below me, the guttural *thud-thud-thud* of the helicopter's blades above me. Each time it seemed that there was going to be a chance for me to land – each time I could feel Chuck start to lower the winch – the yacht would suddenly dart sideways, and the vast mast would wave at me, as if beckoning me down to my doom. Finally he called down on the radio: 'No. This is not happening, we can't achieve it.'

It takes a strong person to realize that we can't always achieve our objective. Our will to complete a task is so strong that we'll want to keep on trying till we've nothing left, but it's right there's someone to stand back, be the one outsider looking in at the crew's limits, and decide whether or not the task is a feasible one, or if the patient would be better served waiting for the lifeboat to come out. On that occasion, I thought, thank God for that – I was about to get written off, I reckon. So they got me back in and we spoke to the Falmouth Coastguard and told them the boat was now steaming toward Land's End; they said the lifeboat's coming out to meet them and that they'd call us if they needed more help, but that the yacht's crew were happy with the casualty's stability, that his injury was not life-threatening, and we were able to return to base. I was very grateful for that decision then.

Of course, when I got back to base we discussed the job – what had gone wrong, what else we might have tried – and Dave Rigg told me about a similar sort of job that had happened to him. It was a job out in the Atlantic, about 120 miles offshore, to a thirty-foot yacht, with a single yachtsman on board. It was a late-afternoon call from Kinloss so by the time they were on scene it had gone from day to night. Dave was operating the winch that time as the seas were particularly rough. He lowered the other crewman, 'Kidney' Hatch, on to the deck but when Kidney reached it the exaggerated movements of the boat in water made him almost immediately and quite violently seasick. Dave himself then had to go down to the boat; first he lowered a highline and was then winched down, Kidney struggling through his seasickness in order to be able to pull Dave in when he got close. However, the waves had worsened, and each time Dave got closer to his target, one moment he would be a comfortable thirty feet above the boat, the next he would be about two feet underwater. This went on – being in the clear air, being swamped by cold Atlantic water – for nearly three quarters of an hour, before finally Dave made it on to the boat. The stench of vomit about the deck was horrendous, not only from Kidney suddenly succumbing to the illness but also from the occupant who'd been ill too. The poor yachtsman remained below decks because he had a neck injury, so Dave decided he needed a stretcher to take the man off the boat. A stretcher was lowered from the aircraft, but then Dave was left with an obvious problem – the yachtsman couldn't move comfortably up to the stretcher himself, and neither Kidney nor Dave were 100 per cent well enough to manoeuvre him onto it. Dave decided then to call for the lifeboat to assist them both on board.

The helicopter, though, had to depart, as it was running low on fuel. With Dave happy to remain on board, the helicopter headed back to the Isles of Scilly to refuel there, while the lifeboat from St Mary's headed out to meet the yacht. The waves continued to rise and rise and twice while waiting for the lifeboat to come out the yacht flipped over so far that the mast hit the water; Dave thought the boat was going to turn turtle until luckily it flipped over and righted itself. 'About fifty-foot waves they were. By day at least you've got an idea when the big stuff's coming through, but at night it's even worse because you can't see them coming.' The lifeboat pitched up some time later to assist; two crewmen decided to come across to help Dave and Kidney bring the stretcher and the patient up, with the idea of then taking charge of the yacht while Dave and Kidney went back in the lifeboat with the casualty. As the boats came close to each other, the two men decided to leap across; unfortunately they didn't quite make it: the pair of them landed outside the guard rails and clung on – only the boats continued to swing together and banged into each other, crushing the two lifeboat crew. So Dave and Kidney now had two more casualties to deal with, and no one to help them move the stretcher. Eventually the lifeboat crewmen recovered enough to be able to help and they switched stretchers over, as our Navy one was too big and bulky, and together they managed to get the man out of the lower cockpit and into their stretcher. As a result of the high winds and seas, which continued to worsen, the yacht lost all radio communications, so they had to signal to the lifeboat that they were ready to get him into the lifeboat. The boat came in close, and after a couple of attempts – during one of which it seemed the yacht might be pulled right over – they managed to get so close 'that we just picked him up, and threw the stretcher with him in into the lifeboat'. The lifeboat crew were obviously brilliant that day, as they set off to return to St Mary's, having been at sea for nearly eight hours by the time they returned.

'I don't get seasick,' said Dave when he returned, 'but it was the closest I've ever felt to being seasick. On the journey back, it was the first time I've seen the whole lifeboat crew, bar the coxswain, being sick. For the lifeboat crew to be sick, it's pretty rough. Even they were saying, we've never seen conditions like this before. I don't want to do it again either.'

It's in the bad weather in the dark that you really earn

your money. I've been on a couple of jobs at night when I've thought, I really, *really* don't want to be here. It was on one of my first long-range boat jobs, and I was on the wire, and I was there for ages because it was just so rough they couldn't get me on the deck. It was well illuminated – we put full white lights on, the boat had put lights on, but we were 180 miles out at sea in the middle of the night. If I'd ended up in the water, who was going to come and save me? And if they did, it was going to be many hours later, so what chance was there I'd still be alive? If I was out of luck I would be out of luck, that would be it, game over. Gav Renaud was the winch operator, an Observer, and he was really struggling because of the appalling wave heights – one minute the deck was above me, the next minute it was forty feet below me. It was fifteen yards away and I thought to myself, this is really going to hurt. I think it was probably one of the first times I used PolyCom, the little radio transceiver that goes in our overalls and plugs into our helmets and apart from the extra back-ground noise it's like still being on the intercom – you can listen to what's going on in the helicopter and talk back to them as well. So Gav was saying to me: 'Sorry, mate, we're getting there, we're getting there, I'm just waiting now,' while the left-hand-seat pilot was looking ahead at the waves, trying for the next quiescent period. And finally Gav did get me on the deck, and I got badly smashed about as the deck rose up and hit me as I was being lowered on to it. All I remember is Gav shouting,

'Sorry, Jay, I'm sorry, sorry,' as I went across the deck, disconnected again and got really pummelled. I got up and it really hurt but of course I croaked out: 'Yeah, I'm all right,' because I couldn't admit I was hurt; I staggered to the wheelhouse and this bloke was pretty poorly, with quite a nasty head injury. I managed to get him on deck and I had to double-strop him as well; it was so rough it took us ages to get him off because we were waiting for that same quiet period – I just prayed it was going to be easier coming off than it was getting on.

But hanging there gave me time to think, you see. Lots of things ran through my mind, things that if I was busy, preparing myself to get on board, I wouldn't have had time to worry about – but as I could do nothing but wait for the moment to get down on the boat, I had time to hear my own thoughts alongside Gav's apologies. I didn't want to be there, what happens if the winch gets cut, oh my God. I wouldn't have been so bothered in the daytime but at night it's horrible; I was in that little bubble of light around the bottom of the aircraft, everything else was just darkness, the void. At that range there's nothing else out there, not another boat in sight, not for a long long way. I felt cocooned in my bubble of light – almost protected within it – and I didn't want to think about what might happen if I disappeared from view because outside that halo of light was what would have been, for me, The End. If I'd gone, if I'd fallen out of the light, that would have been it, nothing would have brought me back into its protection. I stared out into the black night while they dithered above me, and I waited for something to loom out of the darkness — that's how spooked I felt. It was an eerie few moments.

We all dread having to go through with something when it starts to go wrong, and the worst night I ever had was when we had to fly out to a shout on a trawler where one of the fishermen had had his testicles crushed in a machine. This sounds horrific enough but it must have been murder for his crewmates to witness, never mind what it must have been like for the man himself — awful, unimaginable pain. It was a horrible pitch-black night, and the boat was about forty miles off Plymouth. The trawler was steaming into port as fast as it could but the sea state meant it was taking ages. A doctor had spoken to the patient over the radio and then spoke to us. 'Yes, this is time-critical, he's got to come off.' So that was it. We always ask if the patient has to come off, how critical he is, because if it's a really rough sea state, there are obviously inherent risks involved. We took along with us on that trip an Observer who was still learning; and as part of his training he was placed straight on as the winch operator for this job, and that wasn't great — we all need to learn, but the conditions were just too testing for him. The aircraft commander decided, once we'd arrived on scene, that it was too rough to put me down.

'Get me down,' I said, 'and when I'm next to the boat we'll see how rough it is and then whether it's achievable or not. If it is, put me on; if it isn't, then it'll have to be a highline transfer.'

But he was adamant. 'No, I'm not happy. What we'll do is we'll send down some equipment, we'll get him off that way.'

Now this was a perfectly viable approach, so we called down on the radio and outlined what we needed them to do. The trouble was the skipper was the only one who spoke English but he was out on the deck. He'd put the boat on the course we'd told him to follow and it was steering itself so he had to run back inside to go on to the radio. The trawler was steering down-sea, which meant that it surfed down the waves, really speeding up as it did so, before it reached the bottom of the wave where it almost stopped.

It was a really horrible night, and we were facing the opposite way to the boat, we were door-to, the boat was coming down the wave and we were flying backwards in this horrific wind, but it kept us Safe Single Engine – it's a term we use to let all in the aircraft know the power available to us at that time. It means that we can lose an engine in the hover or flight and stay where we are because we have enough power to avoid ditching or any problems like that; and this too was an important part of the training that night for the new guy, who was operating the winch. The two of us readied the kit to go down. For some reason I stuck a blue Cyalume on the cable near the hook, just being extra cautious in the darkness I guess. The cable was successfully winched down to the ship with the strop and, with the Captain of the boat dashing back on to the bridge when we needed to speak to him on the radio, things seemed to be going okay for us to winch the patient back up.

However, when the man was in the strop ready to be lifted off the boat that's pretty much when it went wrong. The guy on the winch wasn't ready for this: he wasn't good enough and he wasn't quick enough – he froze. He wasn't reporting the position of the boat, and the height and speed of the waves coming towards us, quickly enough to the pilots – who can't see what's going on of course because not only is the boat underneath them but they're also facing the wrong way – and the boat disappeared down a wave one way while the aircraft dipped in another direction. As the boat went one way, the winch operator, who'd not seen this sort of situation before and so didn't anticipate it as we old hands would have done, didn't pay out the winch cable quickly enough to make up the sudden difference in height – because it happens in a fraction of a second, with the boat rushing off down the wave while we just drifted forwards and out of the way. I watched in horror as the next moment the wire had gone taut and tripped the casualty over the top of the quite high guard rails, when he wasn't expecting it and wasn't prepared for it, and wasn't even looking at the aircraft. There was nobody on deck with him – the weather was too foul and they'd now retreated back inside the bridge. Luckily he was dressed in a survival suit, because as soon as the winch op saw what had happened he did the best thing and yelled out, 'Cut! Cut!' straightaway. My hand rammed down on top of his on the winch cutter, and we cut the cable; that was the first time I'd ever had to do that. We stared out into the rain and the wind; there he lay, having hit his head on his way over the guard rails, face down in the water on a stormy and totally horrible dark night.

My heart plummeted almost as fast as the man fell. I thought, he's dying; the ship was disappearing into the darkness, steaming away, though they obviously knew what had happened, and the Captain started screaming over the radio, panicking like anything; they'd lost sight of one of their crewmates. The Observer was trying to calm him down, while I was at the door, leaning over, and I shouted over the ruckus, 'All right, everyone calm down, shut up. Person in the water, two o'clock, sixty yards.'

The pilot called back, 'Not visual.'

So I repeated, 'For'ard and right, half past two now, sixty yards, blue Cyalume in the water.' And I thanked God I'd stuck that glowstick on the cable because that two pound fifty's worth of plastic is what saved that man's life. I could see even from this distance that he was splashing and flailing about a bit, but he was still face down.

I brought the aircraft above the man by talking

the pilot over; by this point the boat's out there in the blackness somewhere, I've no idea where it is. I turned to the aircraft commander, and said, 'Permission to jump.'

And the aircraft commander said, 'Negative.'

Protocol be hanged. 'He's dying out there, man, he's face down in the water! Permission to jump!'

And he repeated: 'No – denied. You're not jumping in this sea state.'

Obviously what I was proposing was a one-way mission. We'd lost the winch and they'd have had to send out another aircraft – which they were already thinking about doing anyway, that's normal procedure. But there was a boat out there so I was happy I could stay alive – I had my dry-bag on as well: we have to have them on when we fly in those conditions – and keep him alive. Still, my thinking was let's sort him out right now and worry about afterwards later, and I was absolutely livid that he'd denied me, but it wasn't time for an argument then so I said, 'Right, I'm getting the MS10 out, and throwing it out to him.' But then one of the crew made a better suggestion: 'Chuck out one of the single-seat liferafts, Jay' – we carry them behind the seats and they're like backpacks. So I put one on a highline and lowered it down to him. It hit the water next to him and he flailed about, catching it by chance because he was coming round. He grabbed hold of it and it lifted him out of the water a bit but he obviously didn't know what it was; he was clearly groggy. He could have inflated it – it was a dinghy – but he didn't know that: he was half out of it because in addition to the original injury he now had a head injury, poor bastard. So that was a bit better; we had him pretty much tethered to the aircraft while we kept hold of the highline. He was fully illuminated by the aircraft and we could see that he was coming round. The pilot was on the radio to the trawler captain and he steered the boat round to come back to us; once they were alongside the injured man, they opened the fish-loading door at the side of the trawler and although the waves were coming up over them and flooding the deck, they still managed to pull him back out of the water, although it took four of them to get him back on board the trawler. Once he was safely on board we radioed down: 'Right, we're going back for another aircraft,' but they had already turned towards Plymouth and the lifeboat was on its way out to meet them as well, and the decision was made somewhere along the line that we weren't required. It was too dangerous to try and winch him again, and they were only half an hour away now.

It was a horrible mess. I followed up and the casualty was stable in hospital; he had no issues other than the original injury. I don't think the boat blamed us in the end; it was just a horrific night and it was one of those things that can go wrong, an accident that happens very quickly. Afterwards, there was a full internal investigation – what the hell happened there? We all have to write our own versions of the story on an official form and talk through the things we should try and do to ensure it doesn't happen again. The trainee Observer carried on, tried to get his confidence back; he was all right after that, but I think he'll always have bad memories of it.

I know I did.

There was a worse one; worse in terms of the injury sustained by the sailor. It was on a long-range job, too, which means that the duty crew are working without any backup at all. The squadron had a BBC camera team with them at the time; we work quite closely with the media, I've even done jobs with a small camera on my helmet for some shots on the wire. They stay with us for a few weeks and put together some footage for a series on rescues, so they're always keen to get the widest possible variety of jobs so as to make sure the series covers all the work we do. It happened to be the last night the woman filming was with us, and she said that the series was about ready to go to editing now and that they 'could really do with a long-range night job'. Sod's bloody law. The call came through at midnight. Kinloss told us there was an injured bloke in a fishing boat. We could hear the wind howling and the rain battering – brilliant: just what we didn't want. We seem to be getting fewer of the long-range jobs now. In part that's down to better weather-forecasting, so that crews are able to get to shelter when they know the bad weather's on its way. Maybe there are fewer fishing boats out there. Last winter, we only had about four of that kind of job.

When we go out on the long-range jobs we have to refuel on the way, to give ourselves maximum range and time on scene. This can mean – if it's en route – stopping off on the Isles of Scilly. It's about thirty-five minutes out to Scilly. We get there, refuel, then we can go out 200 miles on scene and back, with just over half an hour out there. There's a great guy there who comes out in all weathers to keep the fuel depot ready for us and to charge the tanks. Except on this particular occasion it was some time after midnight and in those circumstances we're expected to do that job ourselves. Dave Rigg jumped out of the helicopter and lined the barrels up. All was going well with the pumping till the wind suddenly gusted, sending litres of fuel all over Dave, meaning that the smell gave him a headache before they even got to the job.

The duty crew had been told that the job, which involved somebody having cut their stomach, was from a Spanish fishing boat. We're always a bit wary of the Spanish or French boats because the call will come through, we're told it's life or death, we get out there and the patient just needs a sticking plaster put on or they're stood there on deck with their bags waiting, ready to go. The crew were expecting that, with the weather being so bad; a young fisherman had had enough and wanted off. So when they located the boat, not to see someone on deck at least let them know it wasn't one of those jobs. The weather had worsened, and the boat – a little speck in the water when they first sighted it – was being tossed around in the sixty-foot waves. Dave's concern about getting on board was lessened only by the knowledge that his Observer, and therefore the winch operator, was the experienced Lieutenant 'Stretch' Hounsome. Stretch was a crewman himself at one time and worked at Prestwick as well as Culdrose, so is in tune with the job the winchman does.

Peering out into the wind and the rain, Stretch and Dave could see the boat had quite an open deck in the middle, with the bridge at the front, and a big A-frame at the back with a little ledge where all the fishing nets were, with guard rails all round the deck. Their first idea was to put Dave down on to the central deck area, so they dropped a highline down on to it and five crewmen came running out from the bridge and got hold of it, giving Dave a bit of stability as he went out of the helicopter and was lowered down to the deck, the highline held in his hand. The waves were so high, with the boat pitching and rolling up to a height of sixty feet, that the helicopter kept its hover at 120 feet – so that Dave could watch the boat below him, up and down, rocking and rolling. And he knew then that however he did get on to the deck it was going to hurt. 'As soon as I went out, the boat dropped away, everything went taut – Stretch was trying to pay out the cable as quick as he could – all these lads trying to pull me in were making it worse – eventually I had to say let go or they were going to rip my arm off.'

The highline parted instead, so Dave started swinging like a pendulum, towards the A-frame, and he curled up into a ball, thinking, this is really going to hurt now. Luckily Stretch managed to move the aircraft clear, working with Shaun, the American exchange pilot, and went upwind. Dave was still hanging there, blown about in the wind some fifty or sixty feet underneath the aircraft, watching the waves washing underneath him, 'and they were massive'. After a few moments, when it was clear that any attempts to carry out the plan as discussed were futile, Dave was brought back on board the helicopter. The plan changed now that Dave had seen the layout of the deck area. 'We'll go for the central area again but don't use a highline, just try and winch me in if you can, a direct winch.' They both knew it was going to be hard, and that in those waves, even with the boat near by, any slip and Dave would be gone for good. He could barely think straight anyway with a pounding headache from the fuel on his overalls; Stretch puffed out: 'It's going to be hard,' but even though Dave wanted to try it his way he didn't want to do anything that Stretch wasn't comfortable with in case it went wrong because Stretch would only blame himself. 'I'll tell you what,' Stretch countered, 'I'll put you on that back end, where the nets are. I'll get you over the guard rails, and just drop you off.' There wasn't much time left for discussion – they only had about thirty-three minutes on scene and they'd already used nearly ten of those by this stage. Dave went out on the wire again and was hanging there for about five or so minutes, while Stretch was waiting for a quieter period when the waves calmed, but it never came. He had to call down to Dave on the PolyCom and say, 'Mate, I'm just going to go for it.' Gritting his teeth, Dave said, 'Right, go ahead.' The pilot ran the aircraft in over the top of the boat and just as they cleared the guard rails Stretch paid out the cable 'max chaps' – that's 200 feet per minute. Dave went down on to the nets hard, disconnected, got the cable away, called up via the Poly-Com: 'I'm on', and then realized his leg hurt. Looking about him he saw there was an anchor tied to the guard rails hidden in the folds of the netting, and he had rammed his leg right into the back of the anchor. 'So I was lying there, clutching my leg. Bloody hell that hurt a bit.' But there was no time to sit about. The boat was riding up and down in the waves with Dave, holding on for grim death as the boat rolled. He had to get down below decks and assess the patient. Nobody seemed to speak English, which made it even harder, but he was led down inside the boat through the fish-gutting area, with fish guts and blood strewn everywhere.

Dave was struggling, his headache still thumping away, the roll of the boat and the smell of the fish guts really getting to him. He knew that he really didn't want to be there, so he thought he'd see the patient and get him fixed up or off the boat as soon as possible. With that one of the fisherman mumbled something like 'Casualty' and opened a door to what Dave told us later looked like a horror film set: 'There was this bloke semi-recumbent, whiter than white, and the whole room round him was just full of blood. The stench of guts and blood was something else, and I realized that the situation was a lot worse than I thought.' The man who'd opened the door stepped over to the casualty, talking to Dave, who didn't understand a word; so the man lifted up the blood-soaked blanket to reveal the casualty had a thick cut running the full width of his stomach, and all his intestines were hanging out.

'And I . . . *pfffff*, it was one of those what should I do moments,' recalled Dave. There was no time for indecision though – the time left on scene was running out. He went back to a point where his PolyCom could contact the aircraft, and called for them to send a stretcher down, urgently. Then he asked to be shown to the galley, where he rummaged around to find some clingfilm. Returning to the injured man, he put the clingfilm over the man's intestines, then wrapped more film tightly round his body. All this time, the man remained almost unconscious. He was put on to the stretcher and as soon as he was lifted up he passed out completely, which was about the best thing that could have happened to him. The bloke was about 6 foot 4 inches and about nineteen stone, a big lad, and Dave wasn't sure how they were going to get him out through the heaps of fish guts and up walkways to the deck, until he spotted a hatch just outside the room they were in. He got the boat crew to hoist the stretcher out from under a hatch with a small crane they lifted the fish nets with. It meant the patient could be kept level, a small comfort but at least something that might help him. They got him on to the deck, and then had to wait for about ten minutes while the winch-hook kept coming tantalizingly close. Stretch was calling down, 'Yes, no, not yet. Oh no, a massive wave,' and all this time Dave was keeping an eye on his watch. ' I realized I had four minutes to get him and me off. This wasn't good.' Finally the stretcher went up, Dave gathered together the man's gear, which his colleagues had brought up from below decks, and clipped himself on to the winch when the hook came down. Stretch pulled him up 'at a rate of knots' and he sliced through the highline, throwing it back on to the deck as he left. 'It was amazing how much better I felt the minute I got off that boat. Even though I was swinging wildly underneath the aircraft, I was off that bloody boat! I didn't envy them boys staying on there and I felt pretty damn awful – I felt quite ill on there. Although I'd forgotten about the fuel on me by that stage I still had the smell of fish guts in my nose.' We're all the same – take us out of our environment and we struggle; put us back in the air, in the helicopter, and we're happy once more.

Stretch and Dave got the patient straight into the back of the helicopter. The BBC woman put her camera down to help to bring him in – one look and she went white as a sheet. Dave disconnected once he was inside the aircraft, took one look at her and said, 'Go on, get out of the way, you don't want to be seeing all this,' but she hadn't seen too much – the blanket had covered most of the worst of it but she'd seen the blood coming from various cavities. Straightaway Dave went to work on him, Stretch slammed the door to and the helicopter – just about within its time and fuel limits – set off home. After they'd been flying for about thirty or forty minutes, the patient's heart stopped. Dave shocked him with the defibrillator five times, and after another half an hour turned to Stretch and said, 'How long have we got to get back?' And the answer was nearly another hour, so Dave called it: 'He's gone, I'm afraid.' They learned later that he'd been lying, bleeding, in that room for four hours. 'Well,' Dave said later, 'I was never going to get him back.'

The left-hand-seat pilot looked round when we first brought the man on board and said to Dave afterwards, 'I don't know how you can deal with that,' to which Dave replied: 'Don't look.' Sometimes we need the left-hand-seat pilots to come down and help if things are really bad and we have multiple casualties or a very complex situation, but mostly they stay forward, way out of sight. The right-hand-seat pilot can't see anything anyway as the 'broom cupboard' – a metal block full of electronics – is in the way. Dave and Stretch, when they got back to the Aircrewmen's room, said,

'We have, between us, completed nearly 600 SAR jobs: that, for both of us, was the worst job we've ever done.'

I had yet to face anything like that myself; I'd seen some pretty bad things but as yet I'd not been tested to the limit. That was all about to change.

# PART TWO

# 5. Kyrill

Thursday morning, 18 January 2007, and I was just about ready to go home. I'd been on all night and just had to sort out a few things before setting off. One of them was to attend our regular morning briefing, which takes place at ten past eight every day and which we call Shareholders. We go over any information hanging over from the previous night, any regular MoD info that has to be passed on, we have the latest weather briefing from the Met man and then we just talk through all the admin of the day, who's doing what. It takes place at 8.10 a.m. because the squadron that amalgamated with 771 when we moved into this building was 810 NAS. 771 kept its name because of its standing within the SAR community, while 810, which was the Sea King training squadron, was absorbed within 771. It's the squadron's way of recognizing 810 Squadron and its history. Shareholders is so called because all the people who have a share in the day's outcomes attend: all Aircrewmen, pilots and Observers due in that day, and some engineers too (because they brief everyone on the current state of the aircraft, what's on the stand, what's in for repair, that sort of thing). As well as hearing the latest weather briefing we'll make policy decisions on changes to flight crews or aircraft depending on weather conditions. When I was on the aircraft carrier I had to give Shareholders' briefings every morning, along with Bungi Williams; it's a pain but it's a job that has to be done. Obviously that particular Shareholders, on 18 January, we had a lot of talk about the weather and the conditions around the county. We all knew that it was going to be a busy day and that any calls in, especially those from boats at sea, were likely to be demanding jobs.

Right after Shareholders I had to do my handover as I was going off duty because I'd been at work since the previous morning. I was on duty every other day for a set of six days, twenty-four hours on, twenty-four hours off. Only it's never twenty-four; you've always got to do paperwork, clear stuff up, so it's more like twenty-eight on, twenty off in the end. Once I'd handed over I went to check my dive bag; I used to carry two dive sets and I'd carry out regular dive-set checks on top of all the aircraft checks. I kept my dive bag, which is a big black bag with all my kit in, in the aircraft; lumping that there and back from the dispersal was a right pain in the arse because of the weight. If the duty crew weren't taking a diver out with them they'd take the sets out so as to be able to carry more weight – less weight equals more power, after all. But there were times I could leave it in the aircraft, and today after checking my sets, making sure everything was ready should it be needed, I said to Oz: 'You happy for me to leave my sets in?' 'Oh – yeah, all right.' As the storm was coming in it had started getting very rough out there. Dave Rigg began trying to convince me to do some training work with the boat but one look out of the window and it got to the point where we said to each other: 'Oh we're not going to go out in this.'

Those who'd come in that morning were well aware of how bad it was out there; driving into work with the radio on hearing reports from around the country about the chaos. The gales had blown down trees and walls on top of people walking past, so those with radios on knew when they came in the chances were that something was going to happen, because 771 gets called out when the weather's crap. That's the way it goes – if it's a nice sunny day it's unlikely something's going to happen. If it's pretty rough, we know a fisherman's going to get into trouble or a boat's going to sink somewhere.

Today's weather briefing focused on the emerging storm that we'd been hearing about for the last few days, and the chap from the Met reminded us of what we'd been told already, bringing up to speed those who'd only come back on shift after a few days off. Many of us know almost as much about weather patterns and systems as the academics, but we just don't have the same enthusiasm as they do.

'Three days ago, just off the coast of Newfoundland,' and he stabbed at a point on the far, far west of the large map of the Atlantic that he'd called up on his laptop for the daily presentation, 'where what we mete-orologists are calling a "sweet spot" for the birth of extreme weather is, this storm began.' No one seemed that interested in his 'sweet spot' so instead he flipped over to the next image, a swirling satellite picture of the whole of the northern Atlantic. 'Where the cold polar air is meeting the relatively warm subtropical air mass, wavering between the fifty-fifth and sixtieth degree of latitude, a deep low has formed, and it's now mov-ing out and across the North Atlantic.' The next image showed the same satellite picture but it was overlaid with isobars in thick parallel batches. 'A strong wind is moving at the front of the storm thanks to the pressure to the south and south-west of the centre. Air rushing down from the stratosphere is now moving over the cold front, bringing about increased instability as the descending air causes the speed of the storm – from the low up to the high levels – to shift dramatically in the front.'

I don't want to suggest that no one was paying any attention to this but most of us were listening with only half an ear – this wasn't new stuff to us. He stood up and, taking off his spectacles, started waving them in the direction of his maps, which were now showing the more immediately important – to us, at least – image of the Channel south of the Cornish and Devon coast.

'The Germans have named the storm "Kyrill",' he

said. We knew from previous briefings that European windstorms are not classed as hurricanes as they're not tropical storms. In 1954 following the international success in naming hurricanes, Karla Wege, a student in Berlin's meteorological institute at the Free University, suggested that all high- and low-pressure systems affecting Europe should be given names in order to make tracking the systems simpler. In November 2002 the catchily titled 'Adopt-a-Vortex' scheme started, allowing members of the public to buy names that would then be assigned to storms occuring each year. We'd already had Per, Franz and Gudrun that winter. Kyrill, it turned out, was named after a Bulgarian man living near Berlin.

The Met guy continued, becoming more animated as the slideshow moved through satellite images showing Kyrill moving across the North Atlantic, whipping up the sea ahead. 'Severe cyclonic storms like this invariably produce the strongest gusts just before the cold front. This is a horrible combination of factors, especially in the open water at the edge of the Channel,' He demonstrated this by gesturing at the isobars on the map of Kyrill's path, which were as tightly packed as sardines.

'The Met Office has already issued general warnings about the storm,' he continued, and he read out the statement that had been issued three days before: '"The Met Office is warning of a return of severe gales through this week, with winds possibly gusting over 80 mph, followed by a change to much colder weather during the weekend.

'"The focus of concern is turning to Wednesday night and into Thursday, when severe gales are forecast to affect many areas. The strongest winds are likely to occur over much of England and Wales, bringing the potential for more disruption."'

Thanks to the earlier briefings, we were already primed for all the sorts of emergencies that storms like this bring to our part of the world – towns cut off by flood waters, people trapped in cars, fishing boats struggling out at sea, that sort of thing.

'Yesterday morning,' he went on, 'the warning was repeated, and to back it up we also issued a satellite image of the approaching storm, taken from over 33,000 kilometres away. "Forecasters at the Met Office continue to predict a spell of dramatic weather across the UK with gales and heavy rain tomorrow followed by a marked change to much colder weather over the weekend. On Thursday, the southern half of the UK will see heavy rain and the strongest winds with gales or severe gales in many areas. Damaging gusts of 60–70 miles per hour could cause travel disruption and the public are advised to keep up to date with the very latest forecast for their area. Exposed coasts and hills could see gusts as high as 80 miles per hour."'

He put his glasses back on and looked out at the room. 'It's probably going to be worse than that,' he concluded. 'The Germans are already saying this is a "once in a decade" event. Already this morning someone's died; just before six o'clock the Managing Director of Birmingham International Airport was killed when driving into work.'

We all stopped shuffling papers and sat up a bit straighter. This was going to be a busy day, we could all sense that now. I decided there and then that I wouldn't rush home, I'd do my paperwork, hang out in the station for a bit and see what developed. It was likely that if I did go home and things became tough, I might be called back in anyway – so I thought I'd maybe just wait and see before heading off.

# 6. The *Napoli*

The shipping that runs through the English Channel is monitored in a number of places, and the one nearest us is the large Coastguard operation at Plymouth. Their equipment enables them to keep tabs on ships not just in our stretch of the water but worldwide, and they have a hotline open to the station at Kinloss in Scotland, which handles all calls for rescue operations in the UK SAR world. If there is an emergency of any kind, it'll be Kinloss that coordinates the rescue and sends out the instructions to whichever crew it tasks for the emergency – whether it's us, the Coastguard or the RNLI.

But it'll be the Coastguard monitoring traffic that will keep watch on what's coming through our patch and will be responding to the problems that we all faced on that morning.

The *Napoli* – then called the CMA-CGM *Normandie* – was built in 1991 by Samsung Heavy Industries' Koje Shipyard in Korea. She was 275.66 metres long and too wide to travel through the Panama Canal, making her one of the largest container ships to have been built up to that point. After she'd been in service for nearly a decade, the *Normandie* ran aground at top speed in the

Malacca Straits near Singapore, a shipping channel at least as busy as that between Britain and France. It had been fully repaired in the Hyundai-Vinashin Shipyard in Khanh Hoa Province in Vietnam; more than 3,000 tonnes of steel had been welded to the hull. She was then put back into service and managed a few more minor bangs and bumps in the port of Jeddah in Saudi Arabia. In November 2004 the ship, now renamed the *Napoli*, was leased from its owners, Metvale Ltd, by the Mediterranean Shipping Company.

Founded in 1970 by Gianluigi Aponte, the Mediterranean Shipping Company started out as a small ships operator but has now grown into the world's second-largest container shipper, and winner of the Lloyd's Loading List 'Shipping Line of the Year' not only in 2007 but also in five of the eleven years before that. The company runs 270 container vessels and has 20,000 employees. It also has a cruise line, MSC Cruises, which takes passengers to the Mediterranean, Caribbean, South Africa, South America and northern Europe.

Initially the *Napoli* was to cover the route between north-western Europe and the eastern Mediterranean, but in late 2006 she was switched to travel from Europe down to South Africa. It was on one such journey that the *Napoli* came to the rescue of some French yachtsmen, whose boat had come into difficulties in the Bay of Biscay in 'a high sea state and a heavy swell'. The two men were taken on board and given a cabin; *Napoli*'s captain informed the British Coastguard at Falmouth, as was standard practice. The two men were put ashore at Sines in Portugal and the *Napoli* carried on to her destination.

On 29 December 2006, MSC *Napoli* sailed from Cape Town at the start of her northbound voyage; she was four days behind schedule. Her master was Bulgarian, as was her Chief Engineer; the Chief Officer was Romanian; and the crew – on deck, in the engine room and the galley, and with assistant engineers and electricians – were a mixture of Bulgarians, Turks, Indians, Filipinos and Ukrainians, along with two Scotsmen, Nicholas Colbourn and Forbes Duthie. The efficient organization of her owners managed to save some time on her voyage by cancelling the planned port calls at Hamburg and Le Havre. Instead, it was arranged for the cargo that it was carrying, as well as the containers it was planned to load, to be moved to the port of Antwerp instead. Things didn't run quite that smoothly, however. When the *Napoli* arrived at Felixstowe on the morning of 13 January 2007, she was six days behind her original schedule following the failure of one of her four main engine turbochargers. During the passage from Felixstowe to Antwerp, a second main engine turbocharger failed; her main engine governor was also not operational.

On 17 January 2007, at 0812, the MSC *Napoli* left Antwerp bound for Sines, Portugal, with a crew of twenty-six. All four turbochargers were by now working, but the main engine governor remained out of action. Her ETA in Sines was 1800 on 19 January 2007.

The Met Office weather warning issued at 1130 on 17 January was received on board MSC *Napoli*:

> German Bight, Humber, Thames, Dover: Wight, Portland:
> Southwesterly 6 to gale 8 increasing severe gale 9, perhaps storm 10 later. Rough or very rough, occasionally high in Portland later. Rain. Moderate or good.

At 1521 the pilot departed the ship as it set out into the Channel.

On the 17th European windstorm Kyrill reached land on the edge of the Irish coast.

The ship's log entry for 04.00–07.00, 18 January, noted the increasing strength of the storm: 'Vessel rolling and pitching moderately, vessel pounding heavily at times. Sea-spray over fo'c'sle.'

The Met Office weather report issued at 0015 on 18 January said:

> Wight, Portland, Plymouth:
> Southwesterly 6 or 7, increasing gale 8 to storm 10, perhaps violent storm 11 later. Very rough becoming high. Rain or showers. Moderate, occasionally poor.

On the Beaufort scale, a wind strength of force 11 is categorized as a violent storm, which indicates the wind has a mean velocity of between 56 and 63 knots. The Captain of the *Napoli* would have known that this was suggesting exceptionally high waves with a probable height of up to 11.5 metres.

Barely five hours later, at 0505, the Met issued an update:

Wight, Portland, Plymouth:
Southwesterly 7 to severe gale 9, occasionally storm 10, perhaps violent storm 11 later. Very rough or high rain or showers. Moderate, occasionally poor.

The *Napoli* moved steadily forward. In the churning seas, her speed reduced; while she might have expected to make 17 knots with the current output from her engines, she was only able to make 11 knots. The ship, occasionally pitching heavily, was now about forty-five miles south-east of the Lizard Point in Cornwall, and heading into storm-force winds, but was no longer rolling to any significant extent. The size of the ship, though – over two and a half times the length of the pitch at Wembley, and weighing more than sixty-five completely full Eurostar trains – reassured the Captain, and the *Napoli* kept on course. It's not surprising that he thought they were, if not invulnerable, at least unlikely to face anything out in the open sea that would cause them difficulties, and he remained content with the vessel's motion and considered that there would be no damage caused to the forward containers.

During the morning normal life continued as best as possible on the ship, although one of the crew – who'd gone to have a shower – found it difficult to stand in the cubicle as the ship started to judder in the heavy seas. At about 1100, a series of unusually strong waves thudded into the side of the ship, and five minutes later there was an ominous cracking sound throughout the vessel. Alarms in the engine room went off, indicating high levels in the engine room bilges. The Third Assistant Engineer was sent down to take a look at the bottom plates. He saw a pipe spraying water and he quickly shut the pump down; the pipe had broken clean through and the two ends were some inches apart. He noticed a large amount of water sloshing about on the bottom and was on his way back to the Engine Control Room to report what he'd seen when a tank towards the front of the boat's main engine burst open, and a wall of oily water fountained up before flooding back down. Greatly alarmed, the Third Engineer raced back to the ECR with his urgent news.

The Chief Engineer listened and went below to inspect the area for himself. As well as a lot of water swirling across the tank tops and under the bottom plates he saw what appeared to be cracks in the tank tops and what he believed to be a large fracture in the side-shell plating on the starboard side. The usual noise of whirring pumps was replaced by a constant sloshing and hammering on the side of the boat. Fearing the worst, the Chief Engineer switched off the main engine before going back up to the ECR where he rang the Captain and told him that he believed the ship had suffered 'serious structural failure'; he then evacuated the Engine Control Room.

The master carried out the most basic of checks but it was all he needed to do. He stepped out from the bridge, having spoken to the Chief Engineer, and looked over the starboard side. What he saw would have sent a chill through anyone. He saw that the plating on the side of the ship directly below where he was standing was bulging outwards. Worse was the moment that followed, for as the ship rolled to port, he could see below the waterline what looked like a vertical crack. He pulled himself across the bridge as the ship rolled the other way and, sure enough, he could see the same sort of damage on the port side. There was only one thing he could do: the ship's back had broken, she was going to sink, and he and his crew must abandon her.

The Captain and company placed great value on safety and emergency procedures, and the crew had been well-drilled in the use of the equipment and in maintaining everything related to safety on board. Now they were to see why that time and effort had been worth it, as they assembled on the bridge. The crew were instructed to get into their immersion suits and they struggled into the thick waterproof garments, zipping each other in tightly. No one wanted to fall unprotected into the sea, especially in the state it was in.

At 1125 a distress message was sent via MF DSC (Medium Frequency Digital Selective Calling).

A few minutes later, the vessel lost all electrical power, but the emergency generator kicked in and lighting was restored. The crew were organized into the duties required to abandon ship: the bosun and three others went to prepare the lifeboat for launch, while some went to collect bottles of water to take on to the lifeboat with them. With the engines cut and the power gone, the *Napoli* had stopped dead in the water and drifted so that her starboard side was exposed to the battering effects of the wind and the waves.

Once the water had been collected, and the bosun returned from preparing the lifeboat, the Captain conducted a head count. Satisfied that everyone was present, he sounded the emergency alarm – seven long, and one short blast on the ship's whistle – and the crew made their way to the port-side lifeboat. It was a sealed boat, designed to cope with being in rough weather. He then called Ushant Traffic – the authority monitoring marine traffic on the French side of the Channel – on VHF radio and told them that the *Napoli* was going to be abandoned. He gave the position of the ship and then said that he and the rest of the crew were going to take to the lifeboat. By now the crew had boarded the bright orange lifeboat, and the Captain and Third Officer joined them, bringing with them the SART (Search and Rescue Transponder), the EPIRB (Emergency Position Indicator Radio Beacon) and a number of the ship's documents. The Chief Officer told the Captain that all twenty-six crew were now safely on board and the lifeboat's small engine was started; then the boat was lowered the fifty feet into the sea by the Chief Engineer hauling down the remote lowering wire. There were three attachments to the *Napoli* that had to be released once the boat was in the water. The fore and aft falls were dealt with by the bosun but the crewman sitting by the painter couldn't move because, although the lifeboat was able to fit more people in than it currently held, the immersion suits they were wearing ensured they were all tightly wedged together. The Chief Engineer had a knife and he pushed his way between the men to lean down and slice through the painter. The lifeboat jerked free of the *Napoli* and was quickly steered away by the Captain.

Once they had reached a position about a mile and a half away from the ship, the Captain activated both the SART and the EPIRB; now there was nothing else they could do except sit and wait for rescue. The waves pounded at the sides of the boat, sending it tumbling down from the crest of the wave to thud into the trough; the noise of the wind outside the small doorway at the back and the dull sound of the waves about them sent the stunned crew into silence.

With the tossing and turning in the lifeboat it wasn't long before someone was seasick. In that cramped space, which, although meant to hold thirty-two, was crowded with the twenty-six of them, the smell triggered others off, and pretty soon the smell was overpowering. There was a little rooflight that could be cranked open to provide some ventilation but it was pretty feeble. Someone pushed open the small door at the back, but it didn't let much more air in. Instead, when the waves battered the small boat spray rushed in and soon the bottom of the lifeboat was awash in a mixture of vomit and saltwater.

Added to this the crew started to get really hot in their immersion suits. While perfect if they'd been in the cold ocean, crammed into that little space, and bumped up next to each other, they began to overheat. They couldn't even open their water bottles to clear the taste of sick from their mouths as the thick gloves of the suits prevented them from twisting the caps off. The Chief Engineer produced his knife again and cut open the tips of the gloves, allowing the crew to use their fingers properly and to drink some water. Even so, the crew continued to swelter in their suits and in that atmosphere with dehydration, its effects – drowsiness and lethargy – began to settle on them.

The silence in the boat, as the crew awaited rescue, continued.

# 7. Rescue 194

I'd done most of my paperwork – we had to fill in a series of forms after we'd completed each job which we then had to send on to various agencies – and had made myself a tea. The Aircrewmen's room, with some battered sofas and a balcony area outside, is on one side of the kitchen, the duty crew's room the other, at one end of the long corridor that runs the length of the building where 771 is based. On the floor below us are the engineers' offices and stores and the exit doors to the airstrip, as well as the main desk where everyone logs in. All calls into the squadron come in here – including the alarm calls from Kinloss.

Shortly after 11 a.m. the alarm sounded, and the duty SAR crew commander took the phone call. He was told that there was a large vessel sinking in the Channel, that the crew had abandoned ship and taken to the lifeboats, and that it was on the edge of the French zone, but still within UK waters.

Nobody knew at that stage if they were all fit and a well, only that they were all in a lifeboat. We didn't know if any were dead or injured. Kinloss didn't know either as they'd had no communication with anybody inside the lifeboat. So the mission was to go out and locate the ship, find the lifeboat, rescue the crew and bring them back. The squadron's quite a small place and I couldn't fail to hear the details. It sounded big; the original call said there were twenty-six people in the water. So I thought, they're definitely going to need me – I'm the only diver here, I'm ready, I stayed behind when I could have gone home. I rushed over to see Oz Rhodes in the SAR Ops room: 'Do you want me?'

And he looked at me, in a puzzled sort of way, and said, 'No, why?'

'Well, you've got twenty-six people,' I said, 'and I thought they were in the water.'

'No – they might be – we're not sure – they might be in a lifeboat. Anyway, I need every seat I can get. That reminds me – you'll need to get those frickin' dive sets out as well.'

I ran downstairs and out on to the dispersal area and removed the sets from Rescue 193. The pilots, Lieutenant Michael Scott and Lieutenant Olivia Milles, were already out there, checking the aircraft (the pilot signs the aircraft out so technically owns it; they tend to have a better technical knowledge of the aircraft than most of the aircrew – unless they're engineers, like me – because they're flying it and they sit in front of all the instruments. They're in charge of the aircraft and safety, whereas the guys in the back are in charge of the winching and the Observer's in charge of the mission) so I knew that once Oz – the Observer – and Dave Rigg had joined them, they were going to be gone soon. And as I was inside the back of the cab, looking about me, I thought, hmm, they aren't going to get twenty-six people in here, are they? There are thirteen seats; if they just take the one aircraft, they could squeeze them all in, making some of them stand up. It would be a squash, and it would be a close call on how much weight they could take in the aircraft and how much fuel they would have to get back. And if any are injured and are on stretchers, then that's no use at all. So they'll need a second crew out there; right, I'm ready. I legged it to the second spot, put my sets next to the disc where I could see Rescue 194 was being prepped and ran back in (there's always a reserve aircraft ready should it be needed, say, if the duty aircraft couldn't fly or if, as today, there was a pressing need for a backup flight). Rads, Justin Radford, was the second duty crewman, and 'Chuck' Norris was the Observer. 'Sir, you're getting ready to go too, aren't you,' I said to Chuck. 'You'll need a diver if they're in the water, I'm okay to go, I've even got my sets here.' Chuck mulled it over. I could see he was thinking of the weight issue and so was considering leaving Rads behind, and taking me instead, but he must have thought it advisable to have the right cover, because he then said, 'Okay, we'll take you as well.'

Damien 'Daisy' May wasn't on duty that day, but he was in the squadron, day-working. It had been decided that the second aircraft should go out too and they were now pulling a crew together. Daisy volunteered to be the second pilot, alongside Lieutenant Kevin Drodge, and we were all quickly briefed by Chuck before we made our way down to Rescue 194, about twenty or so minutes after 193 had launched. Daisy didn't think twice about volunteering, because, as he said, 'Everyone wants to get involved anyway because that's what we're here to do.' But the magnitude of the task was immediately apparent to all of us, as the wind speed over the hard standing at Culdrose was so strong that it was almost at the very edge of what the helicopter can launch into. Once we were airborne an uneasiness crept in. The weather was truly dreadful and as the helicopter approached the coast and headed out over the sea, Daisy looked down at the churning waves below and thought – and he can't have been the only one on board thinking it – what on earth have I got myself into here?

Rescue 193 had flashed up pretty quickly and reached the scene at about 1150. It wasn't hard for them to locate the lifeboat as it had drifted away from the *Napoli* but with the transponder it was something that could be tracked. The orange paint made sure it stuck out well against the grey-green sea, even though the visibility was very poor, with a mist formed not just from the low-lying cloud that hung over the ocean but also from the spray being hurled constantly into the air. Having taken extra fuel with them – they knew they would need it for the number of people they'd have to rescue – their first job was to assess what they could do and how best to achieve the rescue. The best thing seemed to be to send the highline down to the boat, get the occupants to hold it there while the winch was dispatched, and then for each man to get himself into the strop and be taken off the lifeboat one at a time. At this point they had no idea if any of the men were injured or not. Getting those off who were mobile would allow them to deal with any other cases as they progressed.

Dave got the first highline on pretty quickly. Unfortunately the crew weren't at all *au fait* with the highline technique. Like many people in those circumstances they tied it off on the boat, with the inevitable consequence: as the boat moved away with the waves the line parted – they're only narrow pieces of terylene rope, about 250 metres long. They tried it again with a second one, same thing, they lost the second highline. At that point they discussed things in the helicopter and Dave, being the winchman, said, 'Right, I'll have to go down there.' The Observer, Oz, wasn't too keen on trying to get him on the lifeboat as it was pretty small and rolling about in the water. Dave then said, 'Okay then, I'll put you down,' and Oz was even less keen on that. Then Dave asked if they had heard of Jay's coming along on 194? So they radioed 194; yes, I was on board.

We were travelling along in 194 as quickly as we could in the filthy weather. The wind was as strong as it gets round here, a good 50-, 60-, gusting 70-knot wind, it was that bad. We heard from 193; they'd tried to get a highline on board, hadn't been able to manage it, and they'd lost a few in trying again. Chuck told Oz: 'We've got Jay with us, he's got an extra qualification compared to the winchman in the other aircraft, why don't we have a go when we get there?' We all knew that once someone was on the lifeboat the whole thing became a lot easier, so that's what we aimed to do once we were on scene. I dragged my kit bag in front of me and started to get my kit out so that I was ready if I was called on to go down on the winch. Wetsuit, mask, snorkel, fins, BCD, belt – this is what I'd gone through all those gruelling, painful weeks of training for.

Rescue 193 gave us the latitude and longitude so we didn't have much difficulty locating the scene, and once we were in range we had no problem spotting the little orange thing bobbing about in the waves. They'd drifted a fair way, mostly being blown about from side to side, from the *Napoli*, which was probably less than five miles away, but we only knew that from the radar as the visibility was absolutely horrific. It was all right down to the water, luckily, but a hundred feet in any direction and we couldn't see anything; it was thick pea soup. I couldn't see the *Napoli* at all.

When we arrived, we stayed back a bit, talking, assessing, working out what to do. Rescue 193 had backed away too. The cab seemed quite high up at that point but as yet I hadn't really seen the magnitude of the waves. I knew the sea state was bad because we'd been flying over it but it was only when we were up close to the lifeboat that I realized how high the waves were and what a challenge it was going to be working in that turmoil. It was like flying over an estate of identical houses, with row after row of towering waves, each a couple of storeys high. I knew this was just part of the job, this was what we were all trained to do, but looking out of the helicopter at the waves crashing and rising in spumes high enough for me to feel the spray on my face, I knew this was going to be a really challenging day. Meanwhile Rescue 193 were thinking and discussing plans too. When we'd worked out what we thought was the right approach Chuck spoke to Oz in 193 and told him what we were going to attempt. I would go down on to the boat and then send the crew up one at a time till 194 was full, before moving on to 193. Well, I say 'discussing plans' – really what happened was I was screaming and shouting in the back, 'Get me in there! Tell them to get out of the way! I know how we're going to do this.' Daisy pointed out that all I was doing was giving 193 one more to rescue. 'Thanks for that, Daisy,' I said.

I was fully dressed, and fully happy with how I was going to go about this. The only question was, would I jump from the helicopter into the water as I'd been trained to do as a SAR Diver? Dave told me afterwards that's what he expected me to do and was surprised to see me lowered on the winch and trailed through the water to reach the boat. But I could have spent fifteen minutes swimming to the boat, tired myself out and still not reached it, and then where would we be? I said we'll try this way then, if we can't get close to it I'll jump and try that. Apart from anything else, if I was trailed to the boat, I wouldn't need to wear a full dive set on my back, with air cylinders, which would make me more mobile once I was out of the water. With the weather in this state, Rescue 194 was up and down still, and if I was in the water and they were struggling to pay out cable quick enough I could find myself swimming through water one moment and flying through air the next. If I was at all unstable then I risked banging into the boat, and that really wouldn't be helpful at all.

At the back of my mind was the thought that if we got close enough after the first couple of attempts but still missed it, I'd get as close to the lifeboat as I could and then bang myself off from my QRB – quick release buckle – and then swim to the boat, because at least I'd be in the vicinity. Speed was very much of the essence, and not just because of our fuel consumption.

The one advantage of the bad weather was how it helped with the fuel usage when we weren't fighting the wind. If the wind's steady, then it's not too bad because we can keep a fairly stable position. If it's gusty, then we can't react quickly enough to the wind gusts and we're much more unstable in the hover when we're trying to do the winching. Luckily that day it was a strong but fairly steady wind, which allowed us to use less power, which meant we were burning less fuel, so we could stay on scene longer. The only problem might have been if we were getting low on fuel and flying into wind on the way back, which would make us take a lot longer to get home. If we miscalculated or the wind picked up then the best we could hope for would be putting down in a field – or, in the worst case, not making it to land at all.

That has nearly happened in the past; we had a call-out two years ago when the crew were trying to find some fishermen. They found a couple but didn't have time to find anybody else as they'd reached their fuel limit and had to turn back, but had to go to Ireland because that was closer. They landed when they were already below their safety limit not only for flying over water but even for landing. Had they not made it they'd have been landing on the water, so instead of looking for fishermen the next flight might have been looking for a whole helicopter crew.

At last we were all ready. 193 withdrew and sat off us. They stayed near by so as to be ready to come in at a moment's notice should there be some sort of emergency, and they took the opportunity to film the rescue. We try to film as much as we can, not just for PR purposes but also for training as well. After all, it's not often we operate with two aircraft, so it's useful to see what's going on. People back at base can always say stuff like, 'I'd have done this, I'd have done that,' but if they weren't there they don't know what it was like – which is why we film things. Anyway, as long as we get the people off and they're safe and well, it doesn't matter if it's not pretty – it doesn't have to be.

While I was getting ready to go out of the door, Chuck filmed from 194 and he kept filming through most of the rescue while 194 was on scene – although every now and again he had to put the camera down when there was something else to do, like monitor the waves coming in and get the aircraft up and out of there when a big one was approaching.

The noise of the wind blasting at me the moment I took off my helmet and readied myself by the door was amazing. We're accustomed to the aircraft noise but don't hear it because of the ear defenders we wear. This, though, was like being blasted by the afterburners of a jet fighter. The roar was deafening and non-stop, there wasn't a moment when it went still and you could hear properly. I clipped on to the winch hook and swung out; Rads was standing by and immediately started lowering me down. The wind blew me about on the wire and getting me going in the right direction once I was nearly at sea level was tricky to say the least. I held on with my right hand and pointed the way I wanted to go with my left. This wasn't so much for Rads's benefit because he could see what I needed, but for the pilots, in case they had sight of me. We decided to start me going in at a short distance from the boat, which was standard procedure. I wouldn't want to be too close in because we didn't know what was behind the boat – too close and I might get hit by a propeller we hadn't seen – or where the boat might choose to go with the waves pitching it violently up or rolling it around. It wouldn't do to start the rescue by putting the winchman – me – in danger.

The waves reached up hungrily as if to drag me down with them. One moment I sank into the cold water and started finning like mad, the next I was swinging above the boat, as the wave subsided and the boat sank down into the trough. Finally we saw someone: a guy appeared at the door, waving, as I was nearing the boat. They must have heard or seen us go past, because we'd booted 193 out of the way by then. This farce continued for another minute or two – just approaching the boat was proving to be difficult: each time I got close I was dragged out backwards and up another twenty feet from the water – swim, swim, swim and then airborne. I wasn't bothered, I just wanted to get there – and once I'd been over the top of the boat I could see what the obstacles were going to be, a guard rail at the back where there was a small ledge, hand rails on the top, oh boy, a propeller at the back (it turned out to be a tiny one) – oh this is going to hurt, no, oh. Rads raised the winch just at the right time because I was careering towards the back of the boat, and this time the bloke standing in the door stuck his hand out, trying to help me on board. I didn't want to hold hands with him, because if he didn't have a proper footing my momentum could have carried him overboard.

Finally we tried with me a bit lower down. I indicated

this to Rads, almost on the water this time. I could smell the diesel fumes coming from her engine but knew I was well clear of her prop, and as we came up to the back of the lifeboat I reached out and grabbed the rail on the port side of the boat, just as the cable went tight. This was good news because the cable going tight meant it was safe to release my QRB because I didn't want the hook flying back and catching either me or the rail. As I removed the winch hook, looked up at Rads and nodded to let him know I was on there safely and that he could wind the winch up, a huge swell rose up and I found myself looking into the helicopter, almost, rather than up at it. I bet Daisy was shouting, 'Climb! Climb!' at the sight of that wave coming towards them in the front. The winch safely away, I turned back to the boat and pulled myself over to the starboard side where there was a gap in the railings. The man in the orange-immersion suit reached out and I grabbed his arm and pulled myself on board. Hurrah – stage one complete. He went backwards inside the cabin and I followed him by sliding across on my arse to the door, where I shouted above the wind: 'Hello! *Bonjour!* Everyone all right? *Ça va?*

There was no response inside so I stuck my head in through the open doorway to see what things looked like in there.

# 8. 'One gone – only another twenty-five to go'

I almost recoiled from the hot fetid air filled with the smell of vomit. On the seats around the lifeboat were men squashed up tightly together in their immersion suits, looking pallid and clammy; some turned their faces to look at me, others continued to hang their heads, looking at the floor. One at the back was actually sick at that moment. The floor was covered in water and vomit sloshing about, I could tell from the smell. There was what looked a bit like a high-chair in the middle, where the skipper sat. It seemed to be some sort of steering position, but I didn't see any steering gear, although there was obviously an engine, because I could hear the *chug-chug-chug* outside and I'd smelled diesel on my way in. There was a flap where they could get air in just above the steering seat, and maybe that acted as his viewpoint as well. Beside the door were a couple of men, one of them the man who'd come to help me on board. I turned to him first. 'I'm with the Royal Navy, we're here to get you all off this boat. Is anyone injured?' He looked blankly at me.

Ah. Okay, I'll start again. I pointed up into the air. 'We're going to rescue you, okay?' and I waved my finger round at everyone inside the boat. 'Okay?' This time I got a nod from the man; I assumed he was the First Officer or something like that, but maybe not. 'Is anyone hurt?' I asked, this time indicating a cut by slicing my arm with my other hand. He shook his head. 'Good, good.' I clutched myself and pretended to shiver. 'Is anyone cold?' Again, he shook his head. 'Okay, great.' I pointed out at the sea. 'Did anyone fall in the water?' Another shake of the head.

Now I looked around the interior; there may be nobody injured but they certainly didn't look in a good way. I studied them a bit more closely, focusing especially on those who didn't lift their eyes to look at me. To me, that meant they were really struggling with the effects of dehydration and they should be the ones I got off the boat first. The First Officer by the door, if that's what he was, thought I was checking on what he'd indicated to me, so started saying, 'Everybody okay, sick but no injury.' I thanked him again. It was dark in there – a tiny window in the front and the open one on top, but they let in only a little light to see by. I guess they don't put too many windows in because it must be self-righting. It must have been very hard for them in that tight space, not just because of the smell and the heat, but also all the time they had this noise around them, the constant battering of the waves against the sides and roof, the swishing of the water and sick by their feet, the chundering of the tiny engine, and the 50–70 mph winds whistling round everything. No wonder they were starting to lose it, some of them. The noise had done a good job of isolating them even from each other.

Once I'd mentally got a few lined up, it was time to sort things out with 194. The aircraft had backed away once I was on board – we always try and get the aircraft away from the scene where we're working as people get agitated by the noise. I reached for my PolyCom, so that I could speak to the Observer and winchman and get them to coordinate the highline and the winch, only to find it was waterlogged. Bollocks. Oh well, I'd have to resort to the tried and trusted methods. I waved at the aircraft, certain that they'd be watching me carefully just in case I did lose communications. Sure enough, the aircraft moved forward, and Rads leaned out and waved back to me. I gestured what I thought we should do; get the double strop down, with a highline. I'd get the crew out on to this area on the back of the boat and we'd take them up from there. Rads signalled back that this was all clear and within moments the weighted highline had appeared and was being lowered down to us. I removed my fins and clipped them to my front with a carabiner I'd carried down for that purpose; I wasn't them letting them out of my sight – they were my engines if I went into the water. The boat was being tossed about alarmingly, and I needed my feet free so that I could kneel and press them on the guard rail behind me in order to wedge myself in to keep steady. I peered back inside the boat and noticed some coiled rope by the door. I indicated to the two men sitting there that we needed it moved out of the way, and while they shifted the rope I saw that there were lifejackets at the back of everyone's seats, where they'd discarded them as they warmed up. I picked up the nearest one to me and showed it around the cabin, saying loudly: 'Put these back on, you may need them outside.' After a few moments, they complied, the ones who hadn't taken much notice of me up till that point being nudged by the others to put their jackets on.

What I couldn't see was what was going on in the sea on the far side of the boat. A freight vessel passing the area, the Finnlines *Birka Carrier*, had obviously heard about the *Napoli* and could see the rescue taking place. She sailed close by to try and block the worst of the weather coming at us. Not that I noticed while I was in the lifeboat to be honest – I was only aware of her passing when I saw the video later on.

The highline was now within reach and I grabbed it and started to pull the winch hook towards me as Rads lowered it. Once I had the hook and the strop in my hand, I took hold of the highline and handed it to the man seated by the exit. He held on to it, and I gestured to him to wait for my instructions as to what to do with it. I noticed he had a radio round his neck. I'm not sure who he could speak to on it but I thought it might come in handy if the helicopters had to go and I got stuck out here if we took too long to get them all off. Still, I had to get started, so I pointed to the crewman I thought looked to be in the worst shape. I had no idea what nationality he was but he came forward, a little unsteadily, when I called him towards me. He came out on to the ledge where I was kneeling and I got him down on the platform by keeping his centre of gravity low so that he wasn't too unstable. It also allowed me to keep a firm hold on his shoulder to prevent him slipping off the boat. He did as I told him to, all with gestures of course, and then I got him to lift his arms so I could slip the strop round him, no mean feat when taking into account the size of the immersion suit and the lifejacket around him. I showed him how to keep it firmly in place and said, as firmly as I could: 'Do NOT lift your arms up, keep them by your sides at all times, even when you are in the aircraft.'

When I had him in the rescue strop it was immediately apparent that there was neither room, nor was it a safe enough position to recover two people together, so I waved up to 194 that we'd have to do this one at a time.

The boat underneath us was throwing us up and down, the sea state such that we seemed to spin every time we came near the crest of the wave. The wind caught the spray and flung it across the platform at every opportunity. The constant howling in my ears – I'd removed my hood when I reached the boat – was frustrating. I realized that this short delay was because Chuck was waiting for the helicopter to get close to the boat so that the moment the crewman was snatched upwards the power of the aircraft could help to pull him clear of the water. I watched carefully as the winch cable went taut, before the man was jerked upwards. I wanted to use the highline to demonstrate to my new colleague by the door how to steady the winch cable so that the man reached the helicopter smoothly and safely.

As it was, the man went clear, but only after the sea made one last lunge to try and reclaim him, the water suddenly splashing up at his feet. I started to make a mental note of the waves passing underneath us. Every seventh wave is the largest in the sequence, so I thought if I carefully timed the next one to go I could avoid potential problems of that sort. One . . . I counted to nine before the next swell took us up. If I'd been up in the aircraft, I'd have seen that the gap between each successive wave peak was about 160 yards. Perhaps someone in the aircraft above was watching out for that. Generally the left-hand-seat pilot would be monitoring the temperatures, pressures and height – an extra pair of eyes looking out ahead – and he was also hands-on controls, emergency climb and all the rest of it.

What Daisy was doing was to try and anticipate any problems that might be heading the way of the helicopter. The Observer and the winchman would be concentrating on me down below and the men coming up to the aircraft, the right-hand-seat pilot would be following their instructions about where to position the helicopter, and Daisy was the one looking at the potential difficulties ahead, like where the horizon had gone to. There wasn't a horizon as such because with the wind blowing and the high sea state it appeared really misty so we didn't have much visibility.

Of course, there are devices in front of the pilots which tell them where the ground level is, vital when we're over a sea state like this as the height shifts all the time, affecting not only the distance of the helicopter from the waves but also the length of the cable needed when winching someone off a boat and up to the back of the cab. Get it wrong and the problems can be serious – not just an unexpected dunking for the rescued sailor but potentially a helicopter forced to ditch into the sea. So it's vital that not only do the pilots keep an eye on the instruments in front of them, but also an ear out for the voices calling out from the back – 'Up! Up! Up!'

As I readied the next couple of crewmen to go up to the aircraft, I became more and more aware of how horrible it must have been for them in the boat up till now and how difficult this was going to be. The relentlessly howling wind was probably the worst, but the pitching and rolling in the sea meant we were always unstable and this really began to bother me after a while. I was wedged as tightly as I could be but the door kept slamming against my back as I worked, and every now and again we'd lurch skyward, and I'd suddenly see the tail rotor of the helicopter come towards me before the boys reacted and the aircraft went up. I got the third man ready to leave the boat, but just before I'd signalled to Rads to winch him up the boat dropped down off the wave into a trough so suddenly he was hanging twenty, thirty feet above me, taken away not by the movement of the winch but by the depth of the wave trough. I knew I had to stay calm but I nearly shouted out in surprise – luckily it wasn't alarming for him because I'd had him prepped and he was all ready to go, but as soon as Rads had him inside the cab, I signalled up to the aircraft for them to keep an eye on that happening again to avoid any potential problems. I'd never had to work in waves like this before – we would never have trained in such bad weather – so moments like that were something I couldn't have prepared for. Who knows what he must have made of it – one minute on something solid, not exactly stationary but still solid, the next whisked upwards to hang underneath a very loud helicopter, on the end of a winch wire. At least the noise wouldn't have been too bad, because the deafening sound of the wind would have pushed everything else out of his mind.

After that I put them into the single lift strop before they crept outside the lifeboat. 'Arms MUST be here,' I said, slapping their sides. 'Arms *must* be here.' As they came outside on to the platform they tried to stand up, as I suppose they thought they should do, which was not helpful. I started having to tap their knees and shout out above the wind: 'Down on your knees, on your knees,' slapping them there. 'Kneel down, kneel down,' and I'd tap them. Some of them I really had to force down. I'd pull them down by using the strop because I was holding the single-lift strop and the winch hook, keeping them tight in place.

With the next guy, I made sure the man by the door was holding the highline tightly as he went out over the water, and then while he was raised clear. Even so he still got his feet dipped, because the next wave came across and it was nearly fifty feet high, and with the helicopter at about forty foot above the waves they had to initiate an emergency climb, rising up swiftly to try and get him safely up. Daisy said later that there they were on station with the lifeboat a mere thirty feet below, ready to winch, and then there'd be a trough and the lifeboat might suddenly be seventy or eighty feet below. Luckily for the man being rescued, he was still in his all-in-one survival suit but it must have been unnerving for him, watching that water coming up so fast.

I was starting to tire. Every time the winch went up, I knew I couldn't ask the man holding the highline to pull it back; he was looking exhausted already. So I was dragging a hundred yards of sodden rope each time, and my muscles were starting to tell me this wasn't fun. More urgently, I was sick of the solid metal door banging into my back and after the fourth man went up, I thought, now's my time, while the strop's away, I've got to get this door tied back, because this was my biggest hindrance, and I was feeling a bit of pain from it slamming into me all the time. The highline was in the hands of the chap I thought of as the First Officer – he was just pulling it in or feeding it out as required – so I went to get a piece of rope or something to tie the door back. I found some of the rope that had been inside the life-boat earlier and secured the door with it. At last – now I was properly comfortable for the job and I could con-centrate on what I had to do.

I carried on, selecting the ones who looked weakest, the ones who needed to get off the boat as soon as pos-sible. The next man was in a pathetic state. He was so far gone that he couldn't remember what he was supposed to be doing – he was on his knees one minute, then he stoop up, then he goes to kneel down again – while I'm carrying out all the actions I've done before: I've got the strop round him and I'm doing it up; I'm keeping the winch hook in one hand, giving the thumbs-up, ready for the approach, looking at the aircraft lowering down to us, keeping the cable clear of the guard rails and he's standing up again. I'm holding on to the hook and more importantly his strop, and the snatch comes quickly – he wasn't expecting it and the next thing he knows he's twenty foot in the air.

I'd pulled my hood back over my head so it was still on in case I needed its protection if I fell in the water, but I needed it back right now for sharper hearing – so I could listen. I needed better awareness of what the men inside might be moaning and groaning about, whether they were being sick, or were any of them gasping for breath? It helped to keep me alert. I had to try and tell the difference between someone vomiting up because of the smell and movement, or was he really being sick? Anyway – until I had to be worried about that, there were other things to concern me.

Down came the winch and I readied myself to call the next guy out.

Just then the boat rose on a wave and carried on rising – shit, this one was enormous – and when we got to the top the spray hit me like someone throwing stones. I turned my face sideways and felt like I was lurching forward – which I was, we all were. The boat had reached the crest and was pushed over the edge and down the front of the wave, but as we went down we twisted right around, spinning almost completely about. I could feel the winch tugging in my hand but I wasn't going to let it go, that would have been a disaster. Eventually the boat stopped turning and resumed its customary bucking from front to back, side to side, like some funfair ride, and then I saw that we had a big problem. As we'd rolled and then popped back up the boat had spun quite violently and the winch cable had been caught and had wrapped itself round the hand rails that ran across the top of the lifeboat. 'No, no, this is bad, bad juju, this ain't happening, not now, not good.' It's just as well none of the crew in the boat understood me shouting that into the wind.

The boat was made of a rigid rather than a soft shell, with a walkway, made so that someone could walk down the side of the lifeboat holding on to the metal hand rails at about shoulder height – obviously in calm weather only. Somehow I was going to have to stand up and clamber on to the roof of the boat to unravel the wire. Luckily the guys up in the aircraft had spotted the problem – the cab had followed us round, so they were pretty much in the same position the whole time. The pilots practise that a lot: we do 'dead in the water' transfers from quite large boats, and we can blow them around with the downwash, although not on a day like this because the downwash was probably horizontal to the aircraft, so now Rads paid out extra cable on the wire so as to loosen the tension, while Chuck signalled out from the door. I stood up and slid my hands round to the left to reach the hand rail, then pulled myself up on to the roof of the lifeboat. The roof was narrow enough for me to be able to hold on to a hand rail on either side of it, which let me keep a tight grip with one hand while working on freeing the cable with the other. At first I concentrated on getting the wire cleared because if the boat suddenly dropped in the water again the wire would go taut and maybe pull away like an elastic band, flying back up to the aircraft – and it wouldn't do if it caught in the tail rotor, which isn't far from the winch housing, as it did so. Although I had never seen that happen I had heard stories of such a thing taking place, and I really didn't want to be around it if it did.

But it was when I looked up from what I was doing, as the boat rose in the waves, that I saw the sea around me, and that was when I was able to grasp the true nature of the environment I was in. It was like nothing I'd ever seen before . . . it was hard to see clearly any great distance, but what I could see of it was horrifying, a maelstrom, rough as you like, a scene from an end-of-the-world movie. The sea was throwing itself around like it was in pain, and it made the boat, and me on it, feel very, very small and vulnerable. I've never seen the sea so angry. No time to waste, then; let's get on and get back on the aircraft, get the hell out of here. I slid back down, propped myself back against the door and focused.

The lifeboat continued to run abeam across the waves all the time so I could watch the aircraft trying to keep in position. Each upwelling was quite phenomenal, and some would approach the aircraft, and I could see the guys in the back waving forward to the pilots, 'Quick, climb,' and up they'd go while the sea flipped the boat over to the other side of the wave. I'd lose sight of them for a bit, and then the aircraft would reappear as it came down the other side of the wave to try and find us.

I carried on, the process becoming more straightforward each time as now the men had seen what I needed each one of them to do when they came out on to the platform to be winched off the boat. I kept on ushering the ones that I was picking out in no particular order (apart from what looked like the weakest, as they're only ever going to get weaker) to come towards me while they were inside. I wouldn't go in to help them – I didn't feel seasick myself, but it was now eight inches deep in water and vomit in there and it was obviously not pleasant sticking my head in, although a couple of times I had to get right in there to talk to them. I stayed on the platform as I needed to have the winch hook in my hand; it wasn't just my lifeline, it was theirs as well, so I'd really got to look after it. As I got each one off, and the next one started coming towards me, I'd be looking them over, assessing them so I could see how good or bad a state they were in, what level of consciousness they had, all those things.

By now the survivors were totally exhausted from dehydration, the stress of abandoning ship, being crammed together in this lifeboat, and from the effect of being in the boat, which was massively unstable (it would chuck me across every now and then and I was wedged in). Some of them were completely collapsing as they got to the aircraft door. Meanwhile the constant pulling on the rope was beginning to send fire running up and down my arms and back, but even as I thought: I wonder if anyone here can help me? the First Officer as I called him – who'd been holding the highline – suddenly went downhill rapidly, pitching forward in his seat and slumping sideways. Two problems – first I'd have to get him out and away now, and second I didn't have anyone to operate the highline for me. Would I have the strength to do all the highline work? Retrieving was bad enough but now I'd have to do the work getting them on board too.

As it happens this was nearly the end for Rescue 194 as well. Daisy's main job on board the aircraft was to keep track of how many men from the boat I'd been sending up, because as well as all the other things he was doing he was also calculating weight and fuel loads to see how many more they could take on before they had to set off back to Culdrose. He was forever recalculating, jotting down numbers on the pad on his knee. As more people came on board and the amount of fuel decreased, the aircraft couldn't fly so far. The only constant was that the distance back remained the same. Daisy would assume the wind would be the same strength all the way back, only this time behind them, but he'd still build in an extra 10 per cent factor – 'for the wife and kids', as we say – and then come up with a final figure to be able to get back.

Just to complicate matters there were two other factors that came into play. In a ferocious wind like this, there's the bizarre fact that there is a minimum speed we can fly at to expend the least fuel. It's a bit like driving a car: if it's driven consistently at 50 mph it uses less fuel, and it's exactly the same when flying. So the pilots in both 193 and 194, when they needed to be in the hover, tried to fly at the same speed as the wind – if it was a 50-knot wind and they were flying at 50 knots, they're actually not moving, which meant they weren't using very much fuel at all. It requires delicate flying, making sure the aircraft's speed is adjusted to the wind speed all the time, but it does mean the helicopter can stay in the same place and still be economical with the fuel.

That's on the plus side. On the minus side, flying over the sea causes terrible salt accretion, and Daisy would have had to factor in Rescue 193 losing about 10 knots of speed – an estimate only because there was no way of knowing how much salt because it was so rough, with the wind and spray and the downwash, and also because the helicopter was at quite a low level for a long time, which would most likely mean there'd be more salt on there than anticipated.

Daisy was also reporting back to base. Unknown to me at the time, there were discussions about whether or not they would be able to bring all twenty-six up in just the two aircraft, so a third helicopter – Rescue 195 – was being readied at Culdrose. Passing on this sort of information was a slow process because, although Daisy wasn't able to talk direct to base he could speak to the Coastguard at Falmouth (which surprisingly was having a pretty quiet day, most people having taken a look out of their windows and sensibly decided not to go to sea, while those who were had moored up in port if they could to avoid trouble), but he was mostly dealing direct with the services at Kinloss, thanks to the high-frequency radios we used. He had to let them know that I was on the lifeboat, and that Rescue 194 was taking on passengers, that they were all alive and appeared relatively healthy. Kinloss and the Coastguard coordinate SAR operations so they needed to be kept in touch with what was going on, and they relayed messages – like the preparations for launching Rescue 195 – to and from Culdrose.

I went through the rescue process again with the First Officer, managing to get him aware enough to be stable once in the strop and on the platform, but when he was being lifted up to the aircraft the highline parted. This could have been a real problem but the crew elected to go for a direct transfer. Chuck appeared in the door and signalled that the aircraft was nearly full, they were low on fuel and their time on scene was running out. I knew what they were doing and I just gave them a positive signal, shouting up at the same time: 'Yeah, go for it,' and they lowered the strops to me in one hand, paying out a load of cable, I got it over his head, pulled it tight, and they took him straight off, a clean snap. So the thirteenth survivor was recovered as safely as the others, but the remainder of the crew all needed me to use the highline to get them up again – a job like this demanded we use a highline. Trouble was, they were running short of them now.

Rescue 193's crew had already lost two or three highlines in their initial attempts to get the men off the lifeboat, before they realized that this was a job that could be best achieved with a diver – me – on board. Rescue 194 had now lost a couple of highlines even though I was on board the lifeboat as well. Every now and then a huge wave would come in, the aircraft had to rise up to stay safely above the spray, the boat followed it up initially but then fell back down the wave faster than the helicopter could descend which had the effect of pulling the highline tight. That's all it needed: any kind of straining of the rope would have the same effect – *pop* – it parted, because that's what it's designed to do. It wouldn't do for the highline to have a rigid hold on the boat – so, for safety, the highline isn't attached to anything other than the winch cable.

In this instance, though, what the crew above me didn't know was that I breathed a sigh of relief; not having to drag the wet highline back to the boat, and with a short gap in the work as 194 moved off and 193 took its place, I'd have a short breather. I was knackered and we were only just halfway through.

The two at the back of the aircraft, Chuck and Rads, leaned out to wave goodbye. In the front I could see Drodgey and Daisy doing the same. I waved up to them, giving them a big grin and a thumbs-up. It may have been a huge challenge for me down on the boat but I wasn't going to take anything away from any of the others. If the rest of the team weren't so well-trained and as good at their jobs as they'd just proved, then it wouldn't have gone as well as it had so far. Rads and Chuck and the two pilots had done Rescue 194 proud. I looked at my watch, for the first time since coming on board the boat. I'd been there for nearly an hour. Hell: we'd have to speed up the next few lifts off the lifeboat or 193 would run out of time as well.

Normally when the helicopter moves away from where I'm working, I'd feel a sense of peace and quiet rather than having to close my ears to the noise of the engines and feel the downwash. Not today; the roar of the wind continued unabated and as more and more of the *Napoli*'s crew came off the lifeboat, it became more buoyant in the sea and bobbed about in an even more volatile way. I didn't feel I should be on the aircraft with them, fleeing this horrible place; I was where I wanted to be, doing the job I loved. Bring on 193, I thought, let's carry on.

Rescue 193 had stayed reasonably close by, only about eighty yards away, the aim being to give me and 194 room to work but to be close by in case of any problems. Say if 194 had had to cut their winch cable, which can happen, 193 would have to get straight in there to recover whoever was on it at the time.

I was glad to see the familiar sight of Dave waving down at me. Between us Rads and I had managed well so far but I knew time was pressing and we'd had some problems already – highlines breaking, that sort of thing. Things were only going to get harder from here on in; I was more tired, the crew of 193 had been out there a long time, the lifeboat was more buoyant, the men inside were becoming more debilitated – if something started to go wrong now, then I knew Dave's experience would be a great help.

We signalled to each other how we were going to go about this. Dave had watched what we'd been doing and told me later it was exactly what he would have done himself. He added that he was very happy it was me down there rather than him. He knew that it would be hot and sweaty and disgusting in the boat. He was right, it was: your turn next time, I said.

We got the first guy ready and the highline was dropped down. I pulled away at it, bringing the winch in, and got the strop on him, ready to go. Thumbs-up and he's winched up and away, right to the door of the aircraft. I watched Dave spin him around so that he was facing out to sea and pull him backwards into the cab by using the handle on the back of the strop. I knew that at the same time he'd be lowering the winch with his other hand, paying out cable so as to give him some slack to get the guy safely inside and away from the door. Dave himself was attached to the roof of the cab with a dispatch harness, so that if the helicopter should suddenly roll in the wind Dave wouldn't fall out. Sometimes we have to be careful bringing people in, because they turn to reach out and grab something, expecting to have to steady themselves, as if we're going to just take them off the winch and leave them standing there. Why we have to be careful is because they'll reach out and hold on to you, and we don't want anyone to touch the QRB on the front of our overalls, because if they do grab it and open it – that's what it's designed for, that's why it's called a quick-release buckle – then that's it, that's our lifeline gone. In those circumstances we have to deal with people fast, to prevent an accident, and we punch them gently on the face – it stops them doing anything dangerous in the aircraft. Dave told me – when I was back in 193 and going home – that one of the *Napoli* crew tried this on him. As soon as he was in the aircraft he tried to pull the strop off himself, and when Dave waved his hands off he started being a bit combative, so Dave said, 'No!' and the third time he raised his hands to take it off Dave gave him a quick dink on his nose. He didn't try a fourth time. Dave was able then to steer him back into his seat and strap him in; he'd probably saved the man from falling out, but he wasn't going to know that.

Most people when they come into the aircraft do the dying-fly act, just flopping into the doorway on their backs, waving their legs and arms about. They don't move, it's the old 'I've been rescued' routine, and while that is not surprising, really, given that we've rescued them so they are usually suffering from something, the problem is it's obviously a dangerous environment because if the aircraft banks they can go out. If you keep them attached on the strop you get them into their seat, and only then does the strop come off. We have to manhandle them into a seat and get them safely strapped in as quickly as we can before we remove the strop. When the back door's closed they can move about, but when it's open they have to sit down and be buckled in or attached to a dispatch harness. If they're big, to try and get them up and into a seat is quite hard work, especially if there's a few of them, like with the *Napoli* when there were thirteen of them for Dave to shift – shifting thirteen dead weights was pretty hard work for him. 'Oh come on, now help me out, shuffle a bit on your backside,' he'd been saying, but either they didn't understand or chose not to.

I worked my way through the remaining crew members of the *Napoli*. Still no one spoke to me; they'd grunt if I asked them something, but mostly no one said a word. One of them was a big guy, really tall and strong-looking, and I thought I wouldn't have to worry about him too much, but when it came to his turn it was a disaster.

I pointed inside the lifeboat. 'Okay, you – your turn. Come up to the doorway and wait there.' I don't suppose he understood me but he could follow the pattern everyone else had set. Except he didn't; quite a few of the men had little carrier bags with them – that was their life's history, perhaps, their most important belongings, and all they'd managed to get off the *Napoli* in time, probably – so I took the view that if they could hang on to the bag on the way up to the aircraft, then it was up to them, so when one guy held his bag up questioningly, I said, 'Fair one, take it with you.' But this huge bloke turned up with a large great waterproof bag, a proper waterproof duffel bag, about the same size as a small man. I said, 'No way,' and I pointed at it, 'No, no, no bag.'

And he stared at me, and nodded. 'Yes.'

I tried again. 'No, no bag.'

He wasn't having any of it: 'Yes,' and he tightened his grip on the bag. I felt sorry for him; this was what he had gathered in a hurry from the *Napoli* to take with him, but I knew there wasn't the room up in the aircraft, it was a luxury we couldn't afford – and if I have to decide between his bag and someone's life, well, no question then. Without warning I punched his hand hard, so that he suddenly let go of the bag in surprise, and he wasn't very happy about it but I didn't give him time to react and instead pulled him forward to put the rescue strop on him, which I slipped over his head, and then ushered him outside. He seemed kind of out of it; he was probably severely dehydrated, which led to him having a slightly lowered level of consciousness. He hadn't really responded well to my shouting at him, punching him in the hand to tell him there was no way he was taking this huge bag, that it was compromising his safety. I kept talking to him as I brought him out on to the platform: 'Okay, you're fine out here, keep low, keep your balance,' saying whatever came into my head but keeping it modulated so as to try and calm him. I needed him to be safe out here; that meant getting the strop on him – done – and for him to keep a low centre of gravity – even more important given his size. As he came out on to the platform I tapped his knees, saying, 'Kneel down. Down.' But he wouldn't get down on his knees, and standing up from his seat in the first place probably wasn't the right thing for him but he had no choice if he wanted to get off the boat; he stayed standing, swaying against the movement of the boat and then he must have fainted for he suddenly tipped forward and fell over the edge.

My heart dropped further than any trough. Shit, shit, *shit*: luckily I had a good hold of the strop and the winch hook so although he plunged into the water he didn't go far – my arms felt wrenched out of their sockets though. I was holding tight on the strop – that's what kept him alive, because he was completely unconscious at that point and could have floated away from the boat. The water brought him round after about ten seconds, and he started shouting and flailing about in the water. I was leaning right over the side of the boat. I was approaching the limits of my strength now – I was pretty tired because he was probably number seventeen or something, I wasn't keeping count – and I don't know how I managed it, but I found some strength from somewhere and I hauled him back on board, literally dragged him on, which just about drained every last ounce of energy I had. I got him to a position where the cable was vertical again – or a good approximation of it – and started anxiously looking at the aircraft, muttering through my gritted teeth: *Fucking raise the winch, you must have seen him fall and me pull him in, raise the goddam winch now, now.* I was holding on to him for dear life with one hand, while with the other I was giving them the signal to raise him up; he was flopped on the deck now, and any shift in the boat – which was getting emptier and even more unstable than it had been before – might send him plunging back into the sea.

This all took seconds and in those brief moments I saw the cable tighten and they snatched him off the deck. Dave timed it to match the way the waves were coming in, so the waves were dropping away as he took him, making the lift off the deck clean and quick. I breathed a mighty sigh of relief and watched him all the way up to the aircraft, because you never know what people are going to do – was he going to stick his arms up, and slip out of the strop? – as they go up. Then I would have had to make a decision: am I going to stay here and watch him go, or am I going to leave the boat and swim after him. I think that would have been my decision, I would have swum for him. And I would have been able to rescue him successfully, because I had my harness on and Dave would have lowered the winch down to me and I would have gone up with him to make sure he survived the trip safely; and then we'd have had to start all over again with the boat.

Back on the lifeboat I had returned to my position, my back pressed to the door, huddled in tight to get whatever shelter the small boat could offer, and I'd started pulling the highline back so as to recover the winch when Dave's head reappeared. He mouthed something to me and pointed over the top of the boat, behind me. He moved his arms about – there's a big wave coming, I understood that – so I twisted round to the left to peer over my shoulder.

The sky had gone: in its place was a wall of water, white horses on the top, readying itself to fall upon me.

I shouted, 'Hold on!' though I don't know why as no one had paid any attention to anything I'd said so far, and braced myself, saying to myself, oh, CHRIST as the water hit us and over we went, we just seemed to keep on going, the sea seemed to be coming up to meet me. We were almost at the point where I was face down in the water and I seriously thought: This is it, we're going all the way over. But somehow we didn't, the lifeboat popped back up, and I realized that the men inside the boat must have been really banged about. It was now urgent that we got them off, because any more moments like that and we'd be in real trouble. As more of the men were taken off, the fewer people – ballast in effect – remained in the lifeboat, the more unstable it became.

I got the next man away; I watched as he approached the aircraft door; the wind was blowing so strongly that he was at an angle of about 45 degrees – there must have been some strong gusts to get an adult male in a thick immersion suit to behave as if he were no more than a feather. I realized the crew in the helicopter were getting as anxious as me because the aircraft was trying to descend as low as it possibly could to keep him safe and still get the job done quickly – they were constantly watching the next wave coming in, reacting to it with winch and aircraft. Timing was everything; a couple of the men as they were lifted off were swamped by the waves, even though the helicopter was rising – a big breaker would come in behind us, the aircraft was quickly pushed up and the man on the wire was ripped out of the water and up to the cab. On the platform if I was lucky I'd only be sprayed by the wave as it swept by; otherwise a deluge of freezing water would rush over me, trying to tear me out of the tight spot I'd wedged myself into. To cheer myself up, I started saying to myself, thankfully it's daytime, thank God. At night it would have been a whole different ballgame.

Normally we'd try to take people up to the aircraft smoothly and slowly, so that they weren't alarmed by the experience and didn't do something stupid like waving their arms about. In this situation not only did the aircrew have to react to the next swell, the next wave, but also to the time factor – the most important thing was the safety of both the *Napoli* crew and themselves. No one really had any time to worry about what the ship's crew might think about it. They were probably all pretty much out of it anyway, because they were dangling in the middle of nowhere feeling like crap with nothing to see apart from a helicopter and some massive waves.

Dave appeared at the door of 193 and started waving again. I watched him carefully as he stuck both hands up, all fingers spread widely apart – no, he can't mean that – I looked inside the lifeboat – five people left, five people plus me to get off this boat, and Dave's just told me that the aircraft is going to have to leave in ten minutes. Oh shit no – this was the worst so far, only ten minutes? Right – well, I'm going to do it, we're all getting off here in that time.

Even if we didn't, I decided then that I would stay on the boat. I realized that I was committed to the boat, that I was going to stay on it, that was my conscious choice. I wouldn't go off and leave any of them behind because although I was exhausted I knew I would be okay – they'd refuel and come out to pick me up (I didn't know that Scott Jackson, from the US Coast Guard, Yogi Brunner from the German Navy – both on secondment to 771 – and Chick Pritchard and Malcolm 'Razor' Keen had already been tasked to come out in Rescue 195 to do just that), or I could wait till the Coastguard or RNLI could get a boat out to me, even if that was in a few hours' time. I wasn't going to leave any one of these guys behind, and if that meant there was no time to retrieve me once they were all in the aircraft, then so be it.

I'd been on the lifeboat for nearly an hour and a half and although it had gone quite smoothly – once I'd developed a rhythm for getting the men out of the boat and up into the aircraft. I'd improve every time I did it and understood quite quickly what was best and what was not going to work but this was going to be a testing time. Could I do it fast enough to get them all off?

The aircrew could see my determination as I waved back to let them know I wanted to try and get us all off in time. They were great and helped to combat my exhaustion by dropping the winch hook as close to me as they could, so that I had as little pulling on the weight of the rope to do as possible. Perhaps, too, the *Napoli* crew, or what was left of them, saw the urgency of the situation and they helped me step up the tempo by getting into position for me to slip the strop on them and settle them on the platform as speedily as I was able to, despite the fact the waves seemed to be getting bigger – when I'd first come on to the boat, I hadn't often found myself looking straight into the helicopter, but that seemed to be happening more and more frequently, as we rose up higher each time. Maybe it was because the boat was lighter too – but what had seemed like regular forty-footers now started turning into fifty-footers with even larger ones coming through every now and again.

In my freezing hands I held the highline that stabilized the last man slowly being winched into the helicopter. As the wave forced the boat upwards, the rising water rose about the man's feet, the sea making one last effort to claim him before it sank back down.

The water fell in sheets off his protective suit, leaving him exposed to the howling wind, dangling on the cable as it was winched into the aircraft.

The wind whipped spray like needles into my face. The boat lurched sideways as another forty-footer soared from beneath us, pushing the lifeboat swiftly up to meet the whirling rotor blades above me – any closer and I'd be looking the pilot in the eye. I'd long ago lost the use of my radio – the water had seen to that – and Dave's frantic signalling mirrored my own as I waved back up to him. I needed to get off this lifeboat soon – I was being thrown all over the place now as, with all the twenty-six crew safely on board Rescue 193 and Rescue 194, the boat was being tossed about like a cork in a dishwasher. As a platform for a rescue it'd been un-stable to begin with but now it was positively dangerous. I was pressed up against some metal bars at the back of the boat, to my side was the open doorway beyond which the crewmen of the *Napoli* had taken shelter from their sinking ship. The stench of their vomit pen-etrated even across the ferocious wind, and throughout the whole rescue I'd avoided the reeking, claustropho-bic interior.

The man on the cable was now close to the doorway of the helicopter. Blinking through the heavy spray, I watched Dave spin the figure round so that he had his back to the aircraft, then grab the strop that held the sailor safely on the cable high above the sea, before pulling him into the sanctuary of the waiting aircraft.

When I next saw Dave, it would be with the strop empty, ready to lower it down for me. I begin to gather the highline in my hands, ready to pull as hard as I could to bring the winch safely down to me. As I did so, I turned my head to the left to take one last look inside the lifeboat, just to check that nothing – no one – was left behind. The smell from the eight-inch-deep mixture of vomit and seawater was atrocious but right then, with the boat being thrown up and down by the waves, and the wind pummelling me with spray, I didn't really notice.

I was too tired to notice much, to be honest. As the adrenaline that had kept me going wore off, I realized that I'd never been so tired in all my life. I'd been on that boat a long time now, pulling the winch cable down, often through the heavy waves, getting the next man out from inside the lifeboat and, kneeling him down, getting him correctly into the strop, so as to make sure he was lifted off the boat safely, holding on tight to the highline as he was winched up to the waiting aircraft above, before starting the process all over again. A few hundred yards of steel cable, bowing in the force 9 winds, dragging through the waves, was a tough enough thing to pull in once, let alone twenty-six times. Twenty-seven because now it was my turn to get clear of the boat.

Finally he was in the helicopter, and I was waiting for the hook to come down to me. It was done, over. I was finished, in more ways than one. Thanks to the guys up there, we'd busted the ten minutes we'd had left, but only just – though we'd achieved the safe rescue of all the crew of the *Napoli*. I hadn't left anyone behind; the job was complete. I allowed my eyes to close as I waited for the hook to come down to me, and raised my face to the spray, like it was some sort of benediction. We'd all made it; I'd made it. What a relief.

# 9. Last off the Lifeboat

The winch reappeared below a waving Dave Rigg and we started the laborious process one last time. Down the hook came, with me pulling on the cable to draw it through the wind towards me. Every action tore through my muscles like fire; now that the crew from the *Napoli* were safe, it was as if my body had said, fine, thanks, time to rest now. I had to get a move on, though, as my time here on the lifeboat was up. I knew that Rescue 193 had already busted their 'go' time, would be dangerously low on fuel and were waiting for me so we could all return to base. This stage of a job always feels a bit weird: the job was done, it was time to leave and there was no life left to save, except for my own. I needed to get off the lifeboat so I pulled the hook as quickly as I could down towards me, attaching it firmly to my harness, before grabbing the wire. I shuffled on my knees to the edge of the boat, keeping my balance against the guard rail, before I signalled up to Dave – a rudimentary thumbs-up – and felt the intermittent jerking of the winch wire against me swiftly tighten in the moments before I was lifted up, off that hellish boat, into the gusting gale. The cable above me went taut, and started to sing as the wind played it like an instrument. In the instant before I left the boat I was able, at last, to feel my exhaustion settle around me.

Somehow the moment – and it was only a moment – seemed to stretch out and my senses heightened. The noise of the wind and the waves around me, the unpredictable shifting of the boat under me, the pungent smell of diesel and vomit mingled with the overly warm air coming out of the cabin – all of this seemed intense, as if this very brief period of time was burning itself on to my memory. I was the last on board. All that I could hear around me was the eerie whistle of the wind running through the guard rails and the winch cable, and the loud slap and thud of the waves against the lifeboat. The noise was enough to block out the twin engines of the Sea King above me. Finally, the ocean groaned, the cable gripped my harness and – yanked into the air as if tugged away by a giant, the deck falling away from me – I was on my way.

Never have I felt so grateful to return to the aircraft as I did at that moment when my left hand grabbed the rail and my feet settled on the bar below. Dave paid out enough slack from the winch for me to turn and step into Rescue 193. I shuffled as fast as I could into the back of the helicopter, because I knew the crew needed to get us all moving now I was safely on board. I squeezed myself into a space by the door, at the back of the aircraft, as all the seats were full of silent crewmen from the *Napoli*; with Dave alongside Oz Rhodes, the aircraft commander and Observer, the cab was

full. I nodded across to Oz, and then grabbed Dave's
right hand and his other arm in my left and gabbled
out: 'Nice one, mate, great job, cheers.' After all, I was
pleased with the way things had gone but I was even
more pleased to be going back with them. It was then
that they told me another aircraft had been scrambled
and had only just been turned back, after it was clear
that between them 193 and 194 had the operation
covered.

We turned and headed back inland without much
ceremony. Dave passed me one of the spare helmets –
my own was of course on Rescue 194 – and I plugged
in so that I could hear the crew talking; there was quite
a lot of hushed references to the fuel levels, but I'd
have expected that. Oz stuck his hand out and shook
mine. 'Well done,' he said. A few of the *Napoli* crew did
likewise, mumbling, 'Thank you' at me, but they seemed
shell-shocked – I suppose the events of the morning
had started to catch up with them – and mostly they
continued to sit in silence. I was suddenly elated – the
exhaustion I'd just experienced below had retreated,
and I wanted to jump about, shout, cheer. I had the biggest bloody grin on my face, what a fantastic job, what
a fantastic result.

I sat quietly from then on, looking at the crew we
had picked up. They were all strapped into their seats,
but most had unzipped their immersion suits and as
well as the faintly sweet smell of sick that lingered in

the air I could now smell the heavier stink of sweat. No wonder they were all so exhausted – they'd lost a lot of fluid in the last few hours. They seemed very sullen and withdrawn, a couple leant forward to shake my hand and smile their thanks at me, but most I think were trying to deal with all that had just happened.

The journey home went quite quickly, and I sank back into my seat and ran through in my mind all that we'd just been through. Being exhausted was one thing but I was also pent up with excitement and the after-effects of adrenaline in my system, and as much as I wanted to close my eyes and rest I also wanted to jump about. I wanted something to drink, not just because I was parched but because I wanted to wash the taste of saltwater out of my mouth, only there was nothing on board and I'd have to wait till we got back to the base. I was relieved that I didn't have any job to do on 193 so could sit and listen to the others get on with it. I did notice that they were doing their fuel calculations rather more frequently than normal. I suppose the time on scene, together with the weight and the battle with the wind, meant we were pushing the envelope – in terms of our fuel consumption – just a bit.

We landed over at the Visiting Aircraft Section and Dave and I jumped out to help get the *Napoli* crew down and into the welcoming arms of the team that had been organized to sort them out. The station firemen had gathered to assist us. Although Oz would have radioed ahead, and the other thirteen crew had already been delivered by 194, no one was sure if the group we'd brought in would be able to walk by themselves to the reception committee. As it was, they managed with no problems and we followed them in. I wanted some water or some juice, as I was parched and hot, but this is of course England so all that was on offer was hot tea. So Dave and I got back into the helicopter – the pilots, Olivia Milles and Michael Scott, hadn't turned the engines off – and we made the short hop across to our own dispersal.

Now Rescue 193 was still the duty aircraft and the chances were – with the storm still raging – that the duty crew would be re-tasked and might well have to go out again. The weather was so atrocious it could be one of those days when we might be on the go all day, and I reckoned the crew might be scrambled again because there was so much happening around the county. There might have been a multiple pile-up because a car had run across the road into a telephone pole, or people washed into the sea – which is always a likely one, because even with the weather being as filthy as it was there are always people who take it into their heads to go and have a look at the waves crashing over the sea-walls, and then to their great surprise get washed off – putting themselves and those who come to rescue them into an unnecessarily difficult situation. Therefore, even though I was as tired as I had ever been, I couldn't just get out of the aircraft and walk inside, put my stuff down, get a cold drink and take a shower. It's part of the Aircrewman's job never to walk away from the aircraft without first checking everything's ready to go for the next run. I had to get all my stuff together – which wasn't too much this time as most of my kit was still in 194 – and then carry out the usual tasks of replacing everything that had been moved about, notably the broken and missing highlines.

While I was on board I thought I'd go up front and check the fuel readings for myself. I'd heard a lot about the fuel levels on the way back and I just wanted to see how much fuel we had been carrying, because I knew the aircraft had been out there for a long time, in strong winds, with a lot of bodies on board. I took one look, laughed and had to take a second: I'd never flown on a helicopter with so little fuel. The tanks were just about empty – we must have been flying back on fumes alone; it was amazing to think we could even get the engines moving, let alone keep airborne, like that. We really had pushed it to the limit that time.

I pulled my gear together and then thought I'd better head over to 194 and collect what was left there too, or at least see that my stuff had been removed so that the aircraft was serviceable and that I could pull together everything I would need for the following day. I jumped down from the helicopter and wandered over to 194, parked right opposite the main building, where some of the rest of the squadron were gathered on the balcony overlooking the aircraft and the rest of the station.

What they did next I really didn't expect – at first, I thought they were taking the mick.

I'd been so busy I'd forgotten to ask what had happened to 194 on the way home. I knew they'd arrived safely and that they'd dumped the rescued crew from the *Napoli* in the same place we just had, but I hadn't thought to ask what else had happened – had the crew been re-tasked to Rescue 195, for instance.

What had actually happened was that Rads had taken the video camera off the aircraft as he climbed down. The lads called out to him: 'What's going on? Is Jay still out there?' and Rads had replied: 'Yeah, we've left him on the boat, and he's still trying to get the other thirteen off. Hang on, I'll bring the camera up and you can see the footage.' Once he'd shifted my dive sets out, helped get 194 back on line, and then been de-briefed, he made his way up to the Aircrewmen's room, where he plugged the camera into the TV. The rest of the squadron gathered to watch the raw footage from 194's camera.

About the time that the footage finished, we were touching down in 193. So it was to my complete surprise that the men who'd watched it reacted to what they'd just seen – they stepped out on to the balcony and clapped me. Not realizing what they'd just been doing, I looked at them, shouting up: 'Get lost, you lot, stop taking the mick,' because I thought they were winding me up and giving me a slow handclap for I don't know what, so I carried on yelling up: 'Leave it out,' but the lads kept clapping and called back down:

'No, no, we meant that seriously,' and I thought, oh, that's nice. And I didn't know what to say – it's not often we let our guard down in front of each other because the banter's relentless, but that was something else. I hadn't grasped the scale of what had just occurred because I'd been doing my part of it, and hadn't seen the bigger picture, because although I was involved I hadn't yet been made aware of what the media – and the public – thought of the rescue. The lads' reaction was my first indication that things with this one were different to the norm.

But right then that wasn't in my mind. I wanted to finish what I had to do, then get myself a drink and get clean.

I gathered together all my kit from out of the aircraft and took it through the building, past the engineering section, and turned left straight into the sheds at the back, to the wet room and the dry room, to clean the harness I was wearing and to get spare survival equipment from the SE shed and of course some highlines. I collected the spare SE stuff and took it back out to the aircraft, so it was back on line. Once I'd done that and got everything squared away, I went back into the building and there was a buzz around the place. There were people everywhere, people we wouldn't usually see on the squadron. No one was talking much to me, saying well done or anything like that as they went past, because the squadron was kind of empty in that respect – it was only later I found out that everyone was down milling about in the hangar with the press, and I couldn't see around the corner to the back of the squadron where the hangar was. I went down there and answered all the questions as best I could, from the many interviewers who'd turned up, from local to national papers, radio and TV.

By nine o'clock I'd driven home. Lou, after telling me I looked awful – thanks – knew what I needed: some food and a massage. I was ball-bagged, all my muscles had found new ways of aching, and I sat with her and watched the evening news. There we were again; now that's weird, it has only just happened, earlier today, and now it's some sort of national event, history of sorts. Not just that – I learned things I didn't know, even though I was there.

'The crew included two British cadets, plus seamen from Bulgaria, Ukraine, Turkey, India and the Philippines. Despite the lifeboat being able to hold thirty-two people, the freighter's crew said they still endured cramped conditions. British deck cadet Nicholas Colbourn, twenty, from the Scottish Highlands, said, "There was not much space at all, no leg room and we were cramped like sardines. The conditions were quite actually hot in there because we all had immersion suits on. It was pretty awkward and not very nice."

'The Napoli is carrying about 2,400 containers, although its capacity is more than 4,400. The European Maritime and Safety Agency said the vessel was listed as carrying "dangerous cargo", but the Coastguard said a small proportion of the containers were believed to contain insecticides and pesticides. The ship is now in a stable position forty-five miles south-east of the Lizard and a salvage contract has been agreed. Robin Middleton, leading the Coastguard Salvage Response Unit, said: "The emergency towing vessel *Anglian Princess* and a French tug are on scene. A French salvage team is being transferred on to the Napoli by helicopter and will assess the stability and integrity of the vessel to decide if the vessel can be towed. The current plan is to tow the vessel to a port and discharge the cargo ashore."

'Although the ship was holed in its starboard side, it is listing to port. Falmouth coastguards said that may mean she will not sink. As well as the hole on the vessel's side, the ship also suffered a flooded engine. All vessels in the area are being warned that they should avoid her. The sixteen-year-old vessel is registered to London and was last inspected by the Maritime and Coastguard Agency in May 2005, when officials said it met safety standards.'

That was the first I knew that there was anyone Scottish, an English speaker, on the lifeboat all that time. No way! Why didn't he speak up before? I could have used someone to help me translate for the rest of them, obviously that could have helped me so much more. The language barrier had been quite a problem when I'd had to try and get somebody to man the highline, which was crucial to their rescue. I was astonished – why hadn't he said anything? And there was another

Scotsman too, Forbes Duthie. Two of them – I could have done with their help. Oh well – I guess they were both pretty much in shock from their experiences in the lifeboat so I suppose that explains why they hadn't spoken up.

I was drained of all energy now – the interview process in the hangar had sucked the last bit out of me – so I thought, bed, I need to sleep. At the back of my mind – I didn't want to think about it any more than that – I knew I had to go back on shift the following morning. This had been my day off, so the next day, first thing – what Lou calls 'stupid o'clock' – I was due back at base for another day's work.

# 10. Aftermath

The funny thing is that someone from the public watched the *Napoli* rescue on the news and wrote a letter to the squadron saying that I was someone to be proud of and that he hoped I'd been given at least the day after off. How we laughed.

The *Napoli* job was probably the most rewarding SAR job I have ever done. I look back on what I went through, and if the same job came up now, I wouldn't hesitate – I'd go right back out there. Although I'd been bruised, bashed about, cut up, burned the palms of my hand on the winch cable, drunk half a litre of saltwater every time a wave hit my face and exhausted myself to the point of collapse – I'd do it all over again.

Looking back, I regret only one thing about the way I handled myself on the *Napoli* job – that I didn't jump when I left the helicopter, that instead I was winched down. A proper SAR rescue dive would have required me to jump from the helicopter and swim directly to the lifeboat. But I know there's not much point in thinking like that, not least because if I had jumped and swum through those mountainous seas there's no knowing whether I'd have made it or not, and if I had then maybe I'd have been too tired to complete the mission properly. So maybe it was for the best.

I had a lot of letters from people about the rescue, congratulating me on it; I'd never seen anything like it. It wasn't just from grateful relatives, or anything like that; a lot of the mail was from organizations, as well as some of the most senior people in the Navy. We often get letters after a rescue, but we're advised to have very little contact with relatives of those we've recovered, even if the rescue's been a successful one; mostly for our own sakes, so that we can move on in our minds from something that either was – or had the potential to be – traumatic. The letters that I received after the *Napoli* were nothing like that, I'm glad to say. I heard from the Coastguard, who wrote to tell me that it had been a 'good job'; I heard from Commodore Stanford, the ARCC at Kinloss, Rear-Admiral Montgomery and Admiral Sir Jonathon Band, First Sea Lord at the time. One of my favourites came from Vice-Admiral Waverly of the Fleet Air Arm. He told me some amazing news, but also he had a line in it that made me laugh, as he knew of one of most intense games on the squadron – dice-rolling, which goes on for everything from 'who's going to make the tea?' to more important matters that I'll come to later. 'News has reached me,' he wrote, 'that you've thrown a double six. Following your exceptional performance during the *Napoli* incident on 18th Jan you have been awarded the Queen's Gallantry Medal, and the Guild of Air Pilots and Air Navigators Master's Medal as well.'

I had an inkling that I was going to get some sort of award, which was great, but I didn't know that it was the QGM. I was gobsmacked when I read that; so knocked out that I had to read it several times. The second award – the Air Pilots and Air Navigators Master's Medal – wasn't something I was as familiar with, but when I looked at the list of previous winners, I was absolutely chuffed to see I was going to be on the same list as Larry Slater; that made me really proud. (Larry was the SAR Diver who'd appeared on *This Is Your Life*; the Master's Medal was a really nice surprise, and I was presented with it at a posh black-tie dinner held in the Guildhall in London, by the Guest of Honour, the head of the RAF, Sir Glenn Lester Torpy.)

Thrown a double six – when I read that, I laughed out loud. We spend our time in the Aircrewmen's room, when on duty but concentrating on paperwork, drinking tea, and there's a strict rule about tea-making; tea is made for everyone in the room, and we roll the dice to decide whose turn it is to make it – the lowest score loses and the loser brews up. If one of the dice goes off the table, then only the points from the other one will count; if there's a tie, then those tied roll again. We roll the dice to determine loads of things; it's funny that the Vice-Admiral should know about that.

As well as the formal letters of thanks there were also

some congratulations from former serving Aircrewmen and SAR Divers who were contributors on the 'Rum Ration' messageboard, one used by ex-Royal Navy personnel: I particularly enjoyed the one who thought the 'pilots and mad aircrew diver certainly earned their pay today', as well as the one who had seen the TV coverage, including a clip of me speaking to the BBC interviewer: 'Excellent work, Navy! Interview of the diver typical hero very modest and it was his day off!' I am of course incredibly modest and it was my day off – did I mention that already? And that I was back in work the next day, on a job?

Some of the media coverage was inaccurate, though, and although it might seem harmless it has caused a few problems. The media pegged me as 'a Navy diver' because they saw the wetsuit and that was enough for them – but although my specialization was SAR Diver, my job title is Petty Officer Aircrewman. The issue that caused some real friction though was that I'm not a paramedic, which the BBC announced I was, prompting someone to call in and complain, so setting a few cats among the pigeons.

As well as the individual awards that were made to me and to the two Observers on Rescue 193 and Rescue 194, the crews on both aircraft received an award from the Shipwrecked Fishermen's and Mariners' Royal Benevolent Society, the Edward and Maisie Lewis Award, for 'an outstanding rescue or casevac'. The plaque, which is currently on display at 771 Squadron, states the award is given 'For their skill and gallantry in rescuing twenty-six crewman from the lifeboat of the MCS *Napoli* in appalling weather conditions in the English Channel on 18th January 2007.' And the plaque lists the full crews:

193:

| | |
|---|---|
| Lt Commander Martin Rhodes | Aircraft Commander |
| Lt Michael Scott | First Pilot |
| Lt Olivia Milles | Second Pilot |
| CPOAMN Dave Rigg | Winchman |

194:

| | |
|---|---|
| Lt Guy Norris | Aircraft Commander |
| Lt Kevin Drodge | First Pilot |
| Captain Damien May | Second Pilot (Royal Marines) |
| POACMN James O'Donnell | Diver |
| LACMN Justin Radford | Winchman |

The awards from HM the Queen were officially announced on 9 July 2007: 'Lieutenant Guy (Chuck) Norris and Lieutenant Commander Martin (Oz) Rhodes have both been awarded the Queen's Commendation for Bravery in the Air (QCBA).' My citation, for my 'tireless efforts in assisting those on board the lifeboat in the deeply unpleasant and hazardous conditions', went into some detail about the rescue, using words like 'great courage and determination', 'considerable strength', 'undeterred and calm', all of which made me feel very humble and very proud.

The medal ceremony took place in London that autumn, nearly ten months later. The Navy laid on a Jetstream aircraft to fly a group of us up to Northolt Airport just to the west of London for the presentations because the Edward and Maisie Lewis Award was presented to us the night before I was due to go to Buckingham Palace. The presentation was at Fishmongers' Hall, by London Bridge, and we were staying in a hotel near by, and Louise and my mother, Pat, came up too. Once again there was a fair amount of media coverage of the event, only this time I was in my uniform and we were all together, both R193 and R194 crews. The ceremony was fantastic to attend, and the society praised our 'superb professionalism, teamwork, tenacity and courage'. The lads – and Liv counts as one of them; she's up at Prestwick now – all wanted to get me horribly drunk so I'd have a hangover before seeing the Queen the next day, which obviously I avoided. So instead they spent the evening winding me up: don't mess it up, don't make a fool of yourself, no pressure to get it right then . . .

The formalities of entry at Buckingham Palace coped with, we were separated – Mum and Louise went to take their seats, I was whisked off to be taken through instructions on what we're supposed to do, how we behave, where we go, that kind of thing. We were put into groups and each group was run through in turn; all the people who were about to be knighted – Ian Botham was one of them – were taken downstairs, and those of us who were about to receive medals of some sort were briefed separately. There was a mix of people there, civilians as well as military people. A tall Army colonel – who seemed all of seven foot – took us through the protocols, and he tried to make it light and interesting. It was quite surreal, though, because while I was waiting for my turn I was able to watch the whole thing on TV, and the idea it was happening only a couple of rooms away was odd.

When it came to my turn, number 99, I had to walk forward towards Rear Admiral C. H. D. Cooke-Priest, equerry, or gentleman usher, to HM the Queen. I recognized him and he was clearly used to dealing with nervous sailors like me, coming before the Queen; he knew exactly what to do to settle me down. He was very funny, and set me at my ease, by starting me off laughing. I was waiting in the archway, and I was the very last person to be presented to Her Majesty that afternoon, and there were hundreds of people – the families and friends of those receiving awards – watching me in this enormous ballroom, while on a huge gallery above us a string quartet played all the way through. I'm more than happy to be standing where I am, the last in the line, beaming with pride and anticipation. The occasion has got to someone and the smell of vomit has made its way even here, inside Buckingham Palace, as some poor soul has had a violent attack of the jitters on their way up the stairs, leaving three little pools of sick as we came up. Everyone here today has been lined up and then, in turn, gone to kneel or bow before Her Majesty the Queen to receive their award; and now, after the wait, it's finally my turn.

Alongside Rear Admiral C. H. D. Cooke-Priest I wait and watch others go before me; a highlight is watching Ian Botham being knighted, not just because he's something of a hero of mine but also because – despite the lectures from the immensely tall Army officer – he cocks it up. The Admiral and I have a quiet chuckle as the new knight of the realm forgets to bow to the Queen, so after getting up to leave he stops, turns, hesitates, makes a little attempt at a bow, then wheels again to go in the direction of the Army officer, who by now is madly gesturing at the door that he's supposed to be heading through already. Is that my imagination, or is Her Majesty smiling gently too?

In a moment it's going to be my turn. I mentally go through what I have to do: I'm in my number ones, full dress uniform, which means I've got my medal ribbons across my chest. There's the NATO Medal for the Adriatic (Operation Grapple 1), a UN medal with bar for land operations (three of them) in the former Yugoslavia (Bosnia), then the Golden Jubilee Medal, my Long Service and Good Conduct (LSGC) and – shortly to be added to them – my Queen's Gallantry

Medal. Wearing the uniform clarifies one thing in my mind; just as the uniform shows I'm in the Royal Navy, so I know it means that I'm only here, waiting to get my award, thanks to all those who work in the squadron with me. That's not just the other Aircrewmen, but also the Observers and pilots, and the engineers, all the men on the ground who keep the aircraft flying, fuelled, cleaned and serviced. 771's motto is *Non Nobis Solum* – 'Not Unto Us Alone'. Well, today, I thought, I'm not here alone; all of 771 are here too.

'The Queen's Gallantry Medal: to be decorated, Petty Officer James O'Donnell.'

Time for me to step forward.

It was nice that I was the last person to be honoured; Her Majesty was excellent, we had quite a long chat and she asked me lots about the job.

Finally her hand came out and that was my signal to step back, bow again, turn right, off I went, officially dismissed – that's what they told us upstairs. Normally I'd be able to filter off and go and sit down with the audience, but as I was the last I had to go straight across to the other side of the room, while the big Army colonel continued his mad waving to me, *over here* he was indicating. Nobody had told me where I should go next, so I stood next to him and he said, 'Just follow my orders,' and he marched me round the main room and out by the main doors – because by now the Queen had departed – where we had to step around the three little pools of sick.

I was photographed with my medal with Louise and then interviewed by a BBC crew with my mum. I was very keen to say hello to Ian – Sir Ian – Botham, but we also had to be careful as the three of us had to rush across London back to the hotel, so that we could collect our luggage and get out to Northolt to join the others for the return to Cornwall. Everybody else had already left the hotel to catch the plane and they had to hold it for us. I wish we could have stayed the night, after Buckingham Palace, but we had to go.

Louise and I returned home, picked up the kids, and went back to normality – trailing screaming children about and getting some food ready. I was sitting down, bouncing my son on my knee, trying to quieten him, and Lou's mum and step-dad came round. It was quite a busy evening – they wanted to know what the Queen said – and we decided to watch the TV news, in case they showed Sir Ian being knighted and I could show them where we were standing. There was Sir Ian, a true English hero; and then – amazingly – there was a large photograph of me behind the two newsreaders.

'What!' I lurched forward in my chair.

'Also honoured today was Petty Officer James O'Donnell for a quite extraordinary act of bravery,' said the BBC presenter. We were gobsmacked. There was a lot of footage – me marching forward, and then getting my medal, as well as quoting me as being 'really chuffed'. Then they ran the *Napoli* footage again amid lots of talk of 'swimming through storm-force seas'.

When I was interviewed outside the Palace, I had no idea that this was going to be shown on any news programme, let alone a national one. I thought I'd be at the back of the line given not only that Sir Ian was there but also that Royal Marines returned from Afghanistan were getting medals that day. And then there was a shot of Lou and me together – 'Ooh, there's me,' shouted Lou. The children were decidedly unimpressed.

After that we just had to watch the local news and there we were again. This time, not only did they show me getting my medal but they also had a short clip from the previous night's award as well. And this time the interview was the one with my mum as well as me; and I made sure to mention that I was there for everyone that supported us – the crew – and that it was 'a big team effort from start to finish'.

An unexpected end to an extraordinary couple of days.

The media furore that had followed the *Napoli* rescue was overshadowed by what happened next to the container ship.

After the crew had abandoned it, the *Napoli* had turned north in the high winds and heavy seas and – because it couldn't be safely towed through the busy shipping lanes back to the French side – was beached in Devon in Branscombe Bay on 20 January. This was a contentious decision because this part of the coastline was made a World Heritage Site in 2002. What happened next was played out on national TV: the containers from the ship spilled out on to the beach and a free-for-all followed. Initially it was just people from the area, but as news of the beaching spread 'the hordes were beginning to arrive,' said one local. 'At 2 a.m. it was like Piccadilly Circus.' Those containers that hadn't opened as they'd fallen into the sea or on to the sand, were cracked open and the goods inside removed. BMW motorbikes were shown being wheeled away from the beach; gearboxes, trainers, oak barrels of wine, steering wheels, even dog food were collected and removed. Some people kept warm on the wintry beach by making bonfires of some Bibles destined for South Africa. People who'd packed up their worldy goods to be sent to their new homes watched their TVs in horror as the cases were opened and the contents taken. That the whole episode was played out on national TV probably didn't help. Vans and cars from hundreds of miles away – Manchester and Liverpool, the Midlands and the far north-west – started to appear in Branscombe. A widely held view was that the salvaging work going on was in itself a kind of rescue; that if the containers weren't open and emptied, then the chances were the goods and the TEUs would be washed out to sea in the high tides that continued, following the storm.

Pollution was a serious concern, though the prospect of fuel leaking at the same levels as the big spills off vessels such as the *Sea Empress*, which leaked 72,000 tonnes of oil in Milford Haven in 1996, or the *Torrey Canyon*, which leaked 119,000 tonnes off the Isles of

Scilly in 1967, was minimal. In the event, the leak from the *Napoli* was confined to 200 tonnes. Of greater concern were two of the hundred-plus containers washed overboard that were referred to ominously as holding 'dangerous but low-risk goods'. In fact, one of the containers held battery acid and perfumes and there were small gas bottles for the airbags in cars in the other.

Supposedly 5,000 people a day were turning up in Branscombe – pop. 450 – to see what they could find, and the atmosphere after a while turned nasty. The local National Trust warden, Arnold Fenner – the beach was owned by the Trust – said, 'A group of men tried to stop me going to "their" beach. They threatened to smash my headlights.' The Minister of State for the Department of Transport said in the House of Commons that the 'Police are warning the public that they will use their powers of arrest on anyone attempting to remove articles from beaches.' Not everyone thought Branscombe's new-found fame a problem: the local brewery brought out a specially brewed beer to sell in the local pubs, Napoli's on the Rocks.

But why had the *Napoli* – the largest container ship in the world when it was officially launched in early 1992 – had to be abandoned in the first place? Fundamentally the hull cracked as a result of what's called the 'whipping effect' on the boat. In a storm as extreme as the one seen that January, when the ship is in the trough created by the waves around it – known as 'sagging' – the momentum of the impact when the ship hits a wave reverberates through the ship's hull, an effect exacerbated by the repeated crashing of the ship into waves that are both very large and very steep. As the ship is raised up by the waves, the aft comes out of the water and is sent down by massive G-forces as the wave comes in and crashes on the hull, so pushing it up and away from the aft. When the hull cracked, one of the two Scottish sailors who'd stayed silent when I'd spoken, Forbes Duthie, said, 'I was sleeping in my cabin. I heard screaming. It was like the end of the world.' On such a big ship, it must have seemed exactly that – a cataclysm.

The Marine Investigation Bureau's report identified a number of factors that might have contributed to the accident. Some of these were unforeseen problems – such as the strength of the ship in the engine-room area in the sea state in which the *Napoli* found itself – while some were endemic problems within the container-shipping industry, such as the discrepancy between the declared weights of containers and their actual weights. For instance, one container washed up on Branscombe beach was found to be 20 tonnes heavier than had been declared on the ship's manifest. Obviously, if the ship was carrying more weight than it should have been, or than the Captain even knew about, this would have an effect on its speed and ability to handle the weather, as well as the stacking of the containers so problems caused by shifting in high seas and by weight stresses not being accurately dispersed around the ship would only compound the problems.

As a result of the *Napoli* accident, several similar ships around the world were hastily called in for inspection and modification, to enable them to survive the sorts of extreme weather the *Napoli* had suffered. In Branscombe, the ship was broken up and removed to the shipyards of Harland and Wolff in Northern Ireland to be scrapped, although the last and largest section of the ship – weighing 1,400 tonnes – remained until August 2009 before it was taken off to be scrapped in Rotterdam. Meanwhile the owners of the ship, Metvale Ltd, donated the ship's anchor – weighing 14 tonnes and valued at about £10,000 in scrap metal itself, so no mean gift – to the village, to sit at a spot overlooking the beach, a reminder, as the local council's website quaintly puts it, of the 'ship's extended presence'.

# 11. 771 and the Future of SAR

771 Squadron's SAR work continued and developed into new directions. As well as a good working relationship with SWAST – the South West Ambulance Service Trust – we strengthened the ties we already had with the Irish Coastguard, as the operational area that 771 covers extends far from the Cornish peninsula, across the Scillies, around the western end of the English Channel and out into the Southwest Approaches, to a range of 200 nautical miles into the Atlantic.

January 2007 saw probably double the number of people rescued by 771 compared with the same month in the last two years. In what was probably the last rescue of that month, only eleven days after the *Napoli* rescue, we recovered seven Irish fishermen whose trawler, the *Discovery*, had sunk some 150 miles off the Isles of Scilly. The trawler's crew managed to get into their life raft, but the skipper and first mate spent a couple of hours in the water before they and the others were brought on board a passing tanker, the *Front Defender*. Dave Rigg was lowered on to the deck of the tanker because his medical skills were needed to check on the condition of the men; once they could be safely lifted off the boat, they were put on to Rescue 193 and taken back to Culdrose. This rescue contributed to the high numbers of that month, a total of forty-one people rescued in January 2007 from nineteen callouts. I had worked out that over a twelve-year period we were going on a job once every one and a half days and that over those twelve years we rescued 2,181 people. By the end of 2007, 771 Squadron had rescued 219 people from one sort of emergency or another, whereas in 2006 the number was 180.

Across the UK, in 2007, the RAF and Royal Navy's SAR Ops accounted for 1,817 people rescued, up on the total for 2006, when the number was 1,538. This was from the full range of military SAR stations, that is, eight stations around the country.

Seeing how much medical work we now are expected to give to the people we rescue, it's clear that 771's fiery ex-Chief Diver, Ian Penhaligon, was far-sighted. Ian was one of the men who'd trained me when I'd first joined the squadron; he was also the man who said that the SAR role was changing, and that we should all learn medical skills for the future – and it was he who instituted training programmes that included medical basics. He saw the way things were changing in the world, in particular in the medical world; the duty of care to the patient had become paramount. In days gone by, the squadron was really a lift-and-shift unit: we were there to fly in, pick them up and bring them back. We did very little, if anything, with the people we'd rescued once they were in the aircraft. Now, in part thanks to the relationship we have with the SWAST – which is mainly due to Ian's own efforts – we have learned all sorts of skills that we can employ to keep people going, as long as we possibly can.

There are some who think this is a waste of our time, that we're military people and we should be focusing on that; that if people are foolish enough to jump off cliffs, or sail in bad weather, or travel in large tankers without proper medical cover, it's their look-out. I couldn't disagree more; it's not just that we spend our days learning skills that are applicable in the military world as well; it's not just that we also provide an active branch of the service which people can come to having toured in Afghanistan and continue their training without facing the same high levels of stress; it's not even that we act as one of the best public relations faces of the Royal Navy; it's because we go out most days and save lives for a job, and that's a pretty great calling, one I'm proud to carry out.

Before the current economic crisis, there were plans to make changes in the Search and Rescue world throughout the UK by 2012. The proposal, as it stands at the moment, although with the crunch on public finances biting deep it's not certain this will go ahead as previously planned, is for all SAR helicopter operations – those run by the Coastguard, as well as the military – to come under one unifying authority and the work itself to be put out to tender. For the military branches, this doesn't mean an end to SAR Ops, simply a switch back to where we started – running SAR as a military option only and not the civilian SAR that we've become well-known for.

To prepare for some of those changes, I undertook to teach some basic skills to the Aircrewmen coming through 771 Squadron so that they would know what to do if they found themselves confronted by a situation in which they had to go into the water to carry out a rescue. Using the pool at Culdrose, I have taught men how to approach and work with survivors in the water, whether they're in life rafts or in the water itself. I've taken them through some basic work on parachute drills, and I always stated very clearly that parachutes are killers, bad killers for aircrew, as they can drag a crewman under, enveloping him as he sinks, so if they have to deal with this, they should handle the situation carefully and make sure they keep themselves safe in the process. We worked on how to handle people whether they're conscious or unconscious; we took a look at the different kinds of things the people they would be likely to encounter will be using – were their lifejackets likely to be different to standard Royal Navy ones, were the sorts of seatpacks used out of the ordinary in respect to release levers, that sort of thing; we even covered how to deal with the basic sorts of injuries they might find.

Next we went on to deal with a panicking swimmer trying to climb all over their rescuer, something that was much easier when we were divers – it's a piece of cake if you're on a dive set because you can get your head underwater and still be breathing. If, as is the case with the men I was teaching, they hadn't got dive sets, then you'd have to take each case as it comes, and it may be that things do get to a point where the crewman would have to get physical, would have to punch himself clear because otherwise it's you or him. And it's better if it's you, and him with a biffed nose or unconscious but safely out of the water – that's the sort of training I did with the guys. On the *Napoli*, if the boat's crew had all been in the water, they'd have definitely been panicking, and they'd have tried to fight me to climb up that winch cable just to get out of the water – it's the instinct people have.

Unfortunately the reason I've had to concentrate on teaching the men these skills is because there is no longer a programme that does so.

In late 2007 a decision was taken to dispense with the SAR Divers programme altogether. The SAR Divers training was abandoned, and the recognition of SAR Divers as a specialty within the branch ceased. My skills didn't disappear overnight, but sadly two things did change: I stopped being 'current' on various skills that are required to be doing the job at a top level, and secondly we were no longer permitted to disconnect from the winch cable and swim freely to rescue anyone in the sea. If I did so, then I would be operating outside the rules and regulations – and the protective legal umbrella they provide – of the squadron's SAR capabilities. Tea and medals all round if a recovery went well; but if I was injured while disconnected from the winch, or, worse, through some action of mine a person was injured, then I would be without the legal and financial protection of the service.

I can see why such a decision has been reached, but I would find it difficult to stand back and watch someone struggle or risk their life if I knew I had the skills and the training to protect and save them, even if it meant breaking regulations. It would go against everything that I've learned since joining 771.

Perhaps not surprisingly I expressed these views rather too forcefully when the announcement was made, and in doing so I embarrassed my Commanding Officer, Lieutenant Commander Chris Godwin. Chris is a top bloke and a great boss and I regret that the things I said made his last few months in the job in any way more difficult, because I have immense respect for him. 771 flourished under his leadership and it obviously wasn't his decision to wind down the SAR Divers programme so I shouldn't have been such an idiot – but I suppose it's because I feel strongly about the issue.

Could the *Napoli* job have been completed if I hadn't been a trained diver? I don't know. The weather conditions were very poor and it had already proved difficult for Rescue 193 to get a line down to the men in the lifeboat. If they'd kept on trying, they might well have achieved it, as they're all skilled SAR people, so maybe it could have been done. I'd put it this way: it wouldn't have been impossible to do without a SAR Diver but it certainly would have taken the winchmen above and beyond what they're able to do.

If the winchman is attached to the winch cable he can still enter the water, that's going to happen, but if he's not trained to deal with what he's going to face in that environment – and how others will behave in it – then he's not going to be as effective as he could be.

I've often thought about a scenario like that – going back into a sinking craft to rescue someone – and whenever I look out of the window when it's blowing up a storm it always crosses my mind, and the brief is, we are told to never, ever go back into an aircraft or a closed boat: but I would. I'd have to justify my actions afterwards but if I was back on the surface, and there were people still trapped below, I'd want to go back down. It's just in my nature. It's not that I don't feel fear, but I've never felt any dread before I've gone on a job, I've never felt that – I'm just completely focused on what I have to do and how best to achieve our aims. I know people who ask me about the *Napoli* job want to hear me say that I felt fear, to make me seem more human; but I feel professional. It's not about me, it's about doing what I need to do, talking to the people I need to talk to, getting the job done. The question doesn't get to me but I just don't feel that sense of apprehension: I do what I do because it's part of my training, all in a day's work.

When we knew the SAR Divers were going to be phased out, three of the SAR Divers remaining in the squadron – myself, Bungi Williams and Elmo Pointer – decided that we'd go out on one more training exercise and conduct the last ever fully weighted SAR jumps from a 771 helicopter. We went to Falmouth Bay and did some training with the boat we have stashed there. A few people, who knew it was going to be the last time we'd get to do this, came to watch from a point on the headland. Before we left the squadron we had the most important dice-rolling game of our lives. Who was going to be the last man to jump out of the aircraft? That would have been the day I wished I'd rolled my double six. As it was, Bungi was the winner and he was the last Royal Navy SAR Diver to jump from a helicopter.

Bungi is now Lieutenant Aviation Officer, based on RFA *Fort Victoria*. Damien 'Daisy' May, 'Chuck' Norris, Dave Rigg and Kevin Drodge are still on 771 Squadron. Like the others from that day, I'm not, any longer. I now work on the Merlins for 824 Squadron, and I have to wait until I've finished this tour before I can return to 771 Squadron and the world of Search and Rescue once more.

To all those we rescue, whether they're adrift in the sea or stuck on a cliff somewhere, the familiar Ace of Clubs painted on 771's aircraft must be a welcome sight as the helicopter descends from the skies. The pride I feel, being part of that tradition – the 'Angels in the Guise of Men' – is one of the best feelings I know.

# He just wanted a decent book to read ...

Not too much to ask, is it? It was in 1935 when Allen Lane, Managing Director of Bodley Head Publishers, stood on a platform at Exeter railway station looking for something good to read on his journey back to London. His choice was limited to popular magazines and poor-quality paperbacks – the same choice faced every day by the vast majority of readers, few of whom could afford hardbacks. Lane's disappointment and subsequent anger at the range of books generally available led him to found a company – and change the world.

*'We believed in the existence in this country of a vast reading public for intelligent books at a low price, and staked everything on it'*
**Sir Allen Lane, 1902–1970, founder of Penguin Books**

The quality paperback had arrived – and not just in bookshops. Lane was adamant that his Penguins should appear in chain stores and tobacconists, and should cost no more than a packet of cigarettes.

Reading habits (and cigarette prices) have changed since 1935, but Penguin still believes in publishing the best books for everybody to enjoy. We still believe that good design costs no more than bad design, and we still believe that quality books published passionately and responsibly make the world a better place.

So wherever you see the little bird – whether it's on a piece of prize-winning literary fiction or a celebrity autobiography, political tour de force or historical masterpiece, a serial-killer thriller, reference book, world classic or a piece of pure escapism – you can bet that it represents the very best that the genre has to offer.

## Whatever you like to read – trust Penguin.